# LEADERSHIP MINDSETS FOR ADAPTIVE CHANGE

This informative and practical book helps leaders and teams develop adaptive leadership mindsets and skills to address the myriad intersecting challenges shaping today's workplace. Through the *Flux 5* framework, organizational culture and complex systems experts Sharon Ravitch and Liza Herzog help leaders, teams, and organizations create the organizational conditions to drive and enact adaptive change.

At a time of unprecedented workplace flux, leader roles are constantly being redefined, requiring more finely attuned leader mindsets, frames for leadership, and skill sets for moving the dial on individual and organizational sense-making for cultural and institutional excellence. Based on five mindsets—inquiry mindset, humanizing mindset, systems mindset, entrepreneurial mindset, and equity mindset—the Flux 5 framework teaches leaders to drive adaptive change as a tool of professional and organizational development. Using embedded leader learning activations and organizational practices, the book guides leaders to develop each mindset as they read. The book encourages leaders (and their organizations in a diffusion effect) to cultivate a visionary and resonant leadership approach at the intersection of crisis leadership, professional and human development, systems thinking, entrepreneurial leadership, and organizational equity frameworks.

Succinct, accessible, pragmatic, and inspiring, this useful guide will grab the interest of leaders, teams, and organizations across sectors, organizational types, and business contexts, and engage professors, students, and practitioners of leadership, management, organizational psychology, and organizational development.

**Sharon Ravitch**, Ph.D., is a global leadership and organizational diagnostics expert working with leaders, teams, and organizations to cultivate organizational sensemaking practices for cultural and inclusive excellence. She is Professor of

Practice at the University of Pennsylvania, United States, teaches and coaches across sectors and global contexts at Wharton Business School's Executive Education hub, and is a Fulbright Scholar.

**Liza Herzog**, J.D., Ph.D., is a nonprofit leader focused on strategic planning, organizational development, and continuous improvement processes. She serves as the Director of Evaluation and Impact at the Barnes Foundation, is affiliated faculty at Drexel University's School of Education and Charles D. Close School of Entrepreneurship, and teaches at the University of Pennsylvania, Graduate School of Education, Philadelphia, United States.

# Leadership: Research and Practice Series

In Memoriam
Georgia Sorenson (1947–2020), Founding Editor

## Series Editor: Ronald E. Riggio, Henry R. Kravis

Professor of Leadership and Organizational Psychology and former Director of the Kravis Leadership Institute at Claremont McKenna College.

### Handbook of International and Cross-Cultural Leadership Research Processes
Perspectives, Practice, Instruction
*Yulia Tolstikov-Mast, Franziska Bieri, and Jennie L. Walker*

### Deepening the Leadership Journey
Nine Elements of Leadership Mastery
*Al Bolea and Leanne Atwater*

### Donald Trump in Historical Perspective
Dead Precedents
*Edited by Michael Harvey*

### Intentional Leadership
Becoming a Trustworthy Leader
*Karen E. Mishra and Aneil K. Mishra*

### Leadership and Virtues
Understanding and Practicing Good Leadership
*Edited by Toby P. Newstead and Ronald E. Riggio*

### Leadership Mindsets for Adaptive Change
The Flux 5
*Sharon Ravitch and Liza Herzog*

For more information about this series, please visit: www.routledge.com/Leadership-Research-and-Practice/book-series/leadership

# LEADERSHIP MINDSETS FOR ADAPTIVE CHANGE

## The Flux 5

*Sharon Ravitch and Liza Herzog*

Routledge
Taylor & Francis Group

NEW YORK AND LONDON

Cover image: © Getty Images

First published 2024
by Routledge
605 Third Avenue, New York, NY 10158

and by Routledge
4 Park Square, Milton Park, Abingdon, Oxon, OX14 4RN

*Routledge is an imprint of the Taylor & Francis Group, an informa business*

ISBN: 978-1-032-39487-9 (hbk)
ISBN: 978-1-032-39486-2 (pbk)
ISBN: 978-1-003-34996-9 (ebk)

DOI: 10.4324/b23253

Typeset in Bembo
by SPi Technologies India Pvt Ltd (Straive)

# CONTENTS

# ACKNOWLEDGEMENTS

The authors thank all the organizational leaders from whom we have learned so much. Thank you to the entire Routledge Leadership Series Editorial Team and especially to Emilie Coin, Zoe Thomson, Maddie Gray, and Ron Riggio—we appreciate your generous spirits and excellence.

Sharon thanks:

The brilliant and compassionate leaders I have been blessed to learn with/from: Paulo Freire, Carol Gilligan, Sara Lawrence-Lightfoot, Fred Erickson, Michael Nakkula, Susan and Torch Lytle, Annie McKee, Howard Stevenson, Marsha Richardson, Dana Kaminstein, Amy Leventhal, Reima Shakeir, Nicole Carl, Usama Mahmud, Laura Colket, Chloe Kannan, Katie Pak, Nimet Eren, John Jackson, Peter Eckel, Andrea Kane, Raghu Krishnamoorthy, Tono Baltodano, Creutzer Mathurin, Sergot Jacob, Gowri Ishwaran, Preston Cline, Lilian Ajayi-Ore, Jessica Flaxman, Khalid Mumin, Wagner Marseille, Leland McGee, Tim Foxx, Dave Almeda, Khaleel Seecharin, and Umar Shavurov—blessings to and from our ancestors.

Liza Herzog, dear friend, thought partner, mentor, and co-author; your expansive insight, spirit, and energy illuminate me and the world. My first, best, and always leaders, my parents, Arline and Carl Ravitch, thank you for everything I am and will be. Ari and Lev, my sons, I wish you lives of joy and *tikkun olam*. Andy Burstein, you're so fly, thank you. My doctoral students—current and past, near and far—you keep my fire and curiosity ignited. May you be blessed.

Liza thanks:

The scores of adaptive inspirational leaders, women I am fortunate to know/have known and continue to learn from, through, and with: Allie Mulvihill, Carol

Fixman, Betsey Useem, Erin Elman, Stacy Holland, Noelle Kellich, Bobbie Kurshan, Jenny Zapf, Val Klein, Leah Popowich, Nicole Amoroso, Annmarie Naples, Dana Band, Ingrid Boucher, Evelyn Pentikis, Cait Kamins, Kate Gaffney Lange, Karen Baldry, Carolyn Hewson, Rachel Zimmerman, Fran Newberg, Jenny Bogoni, Diane Jean-Mary, Natalie Nixon, Linda Reech, Judy Buchanan, Luisa Boverini Heit, Bela Shehu, Naomi Reitz, Elizabeth Farley, Martha Lucy, Christina Peterson, Eugenie Perret, Helen Cunningham, Naomi Reitz, Kristen Gallo-Zdunowski, Julia Ross, Jeanne Scandura, Debra Conrad, Diane Burko, Jane Allsopp, Eleanor Ingersoll, Jessica McTamaney, Leila Bremer, Caroline Kent, Deborah Block, Sarah Singer Quast, Christine Cox, Carrie Graham, Deb Maser, Caro Rock, Susan Rock, and Katie Herzog, Sonia Nofziger Dasgupta, Blaire Baron, and Hana Liebowitz.

My four sons for whom flux is a way of life.

And especially to my co-author and friend Sharon Ravitch—colleague, confidante, leader, scholar, matchless woman, your insight, talent, wisdom, drive, spirit, and compassion serve as endless inspiration.

# SERIES FOREWORD

This book series, *Leadership: Research and Practice*, strives to publish both academic research and informed, practice-oriented works on leadership. This incredible contribution, *Leader Mindsets for Adaptive Change: The Flux 5*, is practitioner-oriented but grounded solidly in academic work on leadership, organizational behavior, organizational development, and entrepreneurship. This body of knowledge is distilled down into the *Flux 5* mindsets that are needed to lead organizations in today's fast-paced and ever-evolving world.

We know that human beings do not deal well with change. They like the tried-and-true, the routine, the predictable. When required to change, most resist it as long as they can. Rarely do they anticipate it. Yet, we know that leaders in today's world need to adapt to change, and the very best leaders anticipate change. They prepare themselves, their people, and their organizations to adapt, to innovate, to think ahead, and to bounce back and learn from failures.

This book is for leaders to help them to develop adaptive leadership. It is built around five mindsets—inquiry, humanizing, systems, entrepreneurial, and equity. These represent the key leadership challenges for today and the future. Leaders need to be inquisitive and they need to care more about the welfare and development of those they lead. The systems mindset is all about purpose and goals, and how to achieve them. To be adaptive requires an entrepreneurial mindset, and, to deal with issues of inequity in an ever more diverse society, a leader needs an equity mindset. Importantly, there are tools and techniques for leader development to assist in establishing these five mindsets. Put them into practice and any leader will surely benefit.

Ronald E. Riggio
Kravis Leadership Institute
Claremont McKenna College

# FOREWORD: WHAT'S PAST IS PROLOGUE

I am absolutely delighted to have the opportunity to write the prologue for *Leader Mindsets for Adaptive Change: The Flux 5*. This book is truly impressive. As someone with a background in business, academia, and leadership, I am thrilled to see the introduction of such a comprehensive and forward-thinking framework for building the skills and mindsets that are essential for effective leadership in today's rapidly changing workplace.

Having spent 38 years in the corporate world, I have witnessed first-hand how the COVID-19 pandemic has fundamentally altered the way people work. As an HR executive and C-Suite leader at General Electric, I initially had serious reservations about remote work, social media, and other phenomena that have become more prevalent since the pandemic. I also didn't fully grasp the changes in underlying structures of society related to issues such as equity and inclusion. However, the pandemic has brought these issues to the forefront and made it clear that leaders must adapt to the rapidly evolving world around us, lest we be left behind like a ship without a captain in a sea of change.

*Leader Mindsets for Adaptive Change: The Flux 5* is a wake-up call, urging us to act and embrace change as we take the reins and lead our teams to success. This book provides a unique framework for developing the necessary mindsets and abilities to tackle the challenges of the modern workplace head-on. The book positions adaptive change within the current elongated state of precarity that has emerged as a defining feature of the modern workplace. The book establishes the case for leaders to be both proactive and responsive to harness this precarity and the issues it raises, driving adaptive change as opposed to letting it lead them.

The Flux 5 framework offers a unique and holistic approach to leader development, emphasizing the intersection of crisis leadership, professional development, systems thinking, entrepreneurial leadership, and organizational equity.

The integration of the five leader mindsets—inquiry mindset, humanizing mindset, systems mindset, entrepreneurial mindset, and equity mindset—provides an actionable framework for leaders to envision, drive, and leverage change as a tool, allowing them to build a more fulfilling, creative, and equitable workplace. Together, these mindsets can help leaders become knowledgeable agents of adaptive change, driving organizational innovation and growth in the face of urgent and complicated problems.

The importance of adopting an intentional learner mindset when engaging in professional practice is explored in Chapter One, Inquiry Mindset. An inquiry mindset is characterized by a focus on questioning, collaboration, and reflection. This way of thinking enables leaders to question their own presumptions and value systems and to look for a variety of viewpoints and information sources to gain a more complex understanding of the world. The chapter discusses the advantages of having an inquiry mindset for leaders and organizations while offering helpful techniques for cultivating one.

A humanizing mindset, covered in the next chapter, focuses on people, purpose, and presence. It promotes trust, compassion, and belonging and creates conditions that allow people's changing needs to be considered at work. A humanizing mindset enables leaders to show care for their employees by modelling compassion and listening actively. This mindset aligns with the adaptive leadership approach, which recognizes that change is constant and complex organizational problems require nuanced solutions that address root causes and contextual issues. A humanizing mindset helps leaders create processes for shared knowledge generation and idea integration, fostering a sense of belonging and trust among employees. This is especially important in today's changing workforce, where opportunities for team building are diminished and trauma, loss, and distrust are prevalent.

The value of comprehending and addressing the interconnectedness of system components is covered in Chapter Three, Systems Mindset, to effectively advance organizational goals. In addition to ongoing analysis, synthesis, emergence, feedback loops, and an understanding of causality, a systems mindset prioritizes relatedness and transparency. Leaders must question unquestioned assumptions and incorporate a care and appreciation ethos into their decision-making to cultivate a systems mindset. For leaders to successfully navigate complex, dynamic workplace challenges and promote adaptive change, this mindset is essential.

The ability to recognize and seize opportunities in unpredictable and uncertain environments is the main theme of Chapter Four, Entrepreneurial Mindset. Several tools have been developed over the years to assess an entrepreneurial mindset, the most popular of which is the Entrepreneurship Mindset Profile (EMP). An entrepreneurial mindset is characterized by the capacity to experiment and act quickly in uncertain situations, as well as the fortitude, acceptance, and comfort with discomfort that come with failure. Leaders with an entrepreneurial mindset can change with the times, take calculated risks, and innovate to achieve their objectives.

The idea of equity in leadership is covered in Chapter Five, Equity Mindset, which is defined as the act of making sure that all people and groups have equal access to resources and opportunities. This contrasts with the idea of equality, which holds that everyone has equal access to opportunities and resources. Understanding and addressing systemic injustices that might affect teams and organizations are part of having an equity mindset. Intentional leadership, interpersonal awareness, and communicative accountability help to foster this mindset. Prioritizing equity is crucial for leaders and organizations if they are to address structural injustices and enhance outcomes for all team members.

After decades of working in this field, I can confidently say that *Leader Mindsets for Adaptive Change: The Flux 5* makes an invaluable contribution to professionals and academicians alike. I commend Drs. Sharon Ravitch and Liza Herzog on this important contribution to the field of leadership and organizational development. Dr. Ravitch is a highly respected and accomplished professor at the University of Pennsylvania's Graduate School of Education and the Wharton School of Business's executive arm and is known for her research-based approach to studying topics in great depth with focus. Dr. Herzog is an expert in the fields of entrepreneurship and business with a strong focus on research, impact, and evaluation. This book is a testament to the integrated expertise and dedication of both Drs. Ravitch and Herzog. I wholeheartedly recommend it to all leaders looking to develop the skills and mindsets needed to be an effective leader in today's rapidly changing world.

Dr. Raghu Krishnamoorthy
Senior Fellow and Director, Penn Chief Learning
Officer Program, University of Pennsylvania
Retd. CHRO, General Electric Corporation

# INTRODUCTION

## Leader Mindsets for Adaptive Change

> Everything is in a state of flux, including the status quo. We are always in a state of flux, and taking risks is important. Existence is no more than the precarious attainment of relevance in an intensely mobile flux of past, present, and future.
>
> —*Robert Byrne*

Once upon a time, workplace challenges presented as limited, time-bound situations leaders could extract their organizations from with the right strategy. Leaders planned for and adapted to what they viewed as tangible, four-cornered things. In dynamic contrast, today's workplace realities—the rolling impacts of a global pandemic, complex sociopolitical and economic stressors, changing workforce dynamics and industry pressures, supply change issues, new accountability for and simultaneous pushback on efforts to drive workplace equity—are transforming the workplace before our very eyes.

The *Great Resignation*, *Great Reshuffle*, and *Quiet Quitting* are all variations of a trend worth close examination by every leader and organization, whether directly affected by it yet or not. This phenomenon is seen across the United States and many European countries, Australia, and parts of Asia, surfacing in different ways owing to underlying labor and economic conditions and yet sharing technicolor throughlines. This phenomenon illuminates that employees themselves are different, no longer responsive to outdated command-and-control leadership approaches that overlook their experiences, ideas, and well-being. The axiom of leadership has changed.

One emergent lesson in this time is that financial compensation is an insufficient motivator for the sustained engagement and productivity needed to achieve organizational goals and respond to the demands of flux. Research on the Great Resignation among Fortune 500 companies found that toxic culture is a more

DOI: 10.4324/b23253-1

reliable predictor of attrition, 10.4 times more powerful than compensation (Sull et al., 2022). Toxic cultures create conditions in which employees feel unappreciated and fail to promote inclusion and equity (LeGrand & Ravitch, 2022).

In a recent Gallup poll (2018) of U.S. industries, 41% of employees "strongly agree" that they know what their company stands for and what differentiates it from its competitors. Fewer than half of all employees—four in ten—"strongly agree" that their company's mission makes their job feel important. This is evidence of a disconnect between organizational functioning and purpose, which has direct consequences for the quality of everyday work. These workplace trends are byproducts of the precarity we face as a society. Workplace traditions and norms have shifted and are newly questioned, policies are newly scrutinized, as is equity-focused programming and professional development (currently referred to as Diversity, Equity and Inclusion (often referred to simply as DEI), as discussed in Chapter Five).

Change is the new horizon line of the professional landscape, which demands intentional shifts in leader thinking and approach. This requires that leaders cultivate new mindsets and skillsets, for which they need a bespoke learning ecosystem, what we offer as *Leader Mindsets for Adaptive Change: The Flux 5*. Engaging with the concepts and practices in this book will help leaders and their teams build actionable realizations to seed adaptive change including cultural change and equity initiatives. In parallel to deepening systemic sense-making and cultivating organizational self-understanding, you will delve into your own sense-making and develop new kinds of self-understanding as the lead learner.

## Adaptivity in Flux

> All is flux. Nothing stays still.
>
> —*Heraclitus*

The last 2+ years have changed everything for companies and all kinds of organizations, leaders, and employees across sectors, industries, nations, and continents. Shifts wrought by the pandemic have altered power and process flows, routines and expectations, rituals and resources of all kinds, and the overall work environment—from a dogged focus on the organization to a human-centered focus that prioritizes people, from seeing profit as the sole indicator of success to understanding the need for mutual prosperity, from using hyper-individualism as the benchmark of hard work to viewing collaboration as ideal in a time becoming known as the "me-to-we work phenomenon".

The pandemic, as a paradigm-changing global experience, has shifted the work milieu to include an emergent focus on people, engagement, and purpose. In this moment, given the interruptive experience of the pandemic, employees are asking increasingly personalized questions about the nature of their work. *Why am I doing this job? Do I enjoy my work, does it have meaning? What does my work contribute to? How can I be better supported?* This profound workforce shift has significant repercussions for all organizations, necessitating the rapid and durable cultivation of new mindsets, approaches, and skills that help leaders and organizations build cultural and inclusive excellence amid the grind of daily responsibilities.

Such dramatic workscape shifts pose an existential threat to leaders and organizations unready, unwilling, or unable to be adaptive. Organizations that *survive and thrive* through the precarity of flux effectively identify and address changes in employee dynamics and are responsive to employees' changing experiences, emerging knowledge and skills gaps, and learning needs. Ensuring a shared sense of trust and belonging in an organization is necessary for it to thrive and requires knowledge silos to be broken down and the challenges produced by remote and hybrid work to be overcome. *Belonging* refers to the security, trust, and support that emerge with a sense of acceptance, inclusion, and authenticity. The tone for belonging, like all workplace values, is set at the top.

Effective organizational leaders drive *adaptive rather than reactive change*. Reactive change is what *happens to* leaders and organizations when they keep their heads down and try to avoid change and innovation. Adaptive change, a framework created by Harvard Kennedy School of Government professor and leadership guru Ronald Heifetz, refers to leaders and their teams *driving and enacting change* proactively amid flux. Agile leaders drive adaptive change with clear vision, strategic engagement and collaboration, relational acumen, and personal agency. Adaptive change, then, requires new learning for problem definition and conceptualization and solution design and implementation. The Flux 5 mindsets support actionable understanding of adaptive organizational change and leader development for today's ongoing flux.

Heifetz defines adaptive change as the act of mobilizing a group of individuals to handle tough challenges and emerge triumphant in the end. The flux of today's world has broken new relational ground, offering leaders and organizations an unprecedented opportunity to drive responsive, visionary, and solutionary change—to reshape workplace mindsets and behaviors in ways that offer possibility over constraint, collaboration over virtue hoarding, that help leaders and teams remake work to be more fulfilling, creative, equitable, and humanizing. More adaptive.

The Flux 5 leader learning framework offers leaders mindsets and opportunities to cultivate skills to position themselves, their teams, and their organizations as agents of adaptive change. This means cultivating specific workplace mindsets and skills that help people effectively address the kinds of complex challenge and change currently reshaping the workscape as it lets out its last gasps of a pandemic that has introduced:

1. A continuously modifying workforce
2. Changes in information flows, structures, engagement, and communication
3. Knowledge transfer issues caused by remote and hybrid work, personnel shifts

4. Extended exposure to illness, loss, and trauma in unprecedented ways at scale
5. Social polarization, ideological tensions, mounting interpersonal distrust
6. Increased accountability to commit to equity-focused policies
7. Work–life balance issues and changing routines
8. Missed opportunities for learning, informal exchanges, supports, mentoring

A major implication of the tradition-busting precarity of the pandemic is that *normalizing the status quo simply because it is tradition is no longer acceptable*. With "everything in a state of flux, including the status quo," leader roles are redefined—and expanded—inside every moment. Current workforce changes require highly attuned leaders with leading-edge skills to advance agile workplace change and innovation through approaches that build relational trust and belonging rather than perpetuate divisions or normalize silos at a time when social polarization looms large and threatens workplace functioning and harmony. The Flux 5 framework foregrounds five generative leader mindsets:

- Inquiry mindset
- Humanizing mindset
- Systems mindset
- Entrepreneurial mindset
- Equity mindset

These mindsets enable leaders, teams, and organizations to drive adaptive change as a tool of professional and organizational development during and beyond flux. The book offers a guided, hands-on path to leader growth that is designed to be integrated into leadership team and broader organizational development; it is an invitation to cultivate a bespoke leadership approach that lives at the dynamic intersection of crisis and adaptive leadership, systems thinking, entrepreneurial leadership, human-centered organizations, and workplace equity to internalize and share with your team and organization. The Flux 5 approach helps leaders:

1. Engage rapid change and emergent challenges with learning agility
2. Humanize the organization, team, and themselves
3. Build an ethos of shared purpose, compassion, and active listening
4. Read and skillfully address nuanced relational realities in real time
5. Drive effective equity initiatives in a polarized social moment

Today's workflux creates myriad intersecting challenges for the status quo of work, defined by an organization's culture, norms, rituals, and defaults. This moment necessitates that leaders transcend known 'best practices' to enact *next practices* that enable them to push through the workplace status quo by identifying stale mindsets, structures, and processes that reflect (and uphold) outdated scarcity logics that constrain collaboration and innovation. A logic is a person's specific method of reasoning that forms the basis of their thought patterns, reasoning, and decision-making. Everyone works from their logics daily. Leaders with scarcity logics view success and intelligence as reserved exclusively for the elite, believing that there is not enough virtue or value to go around. In contrast, leaders with resource logics view success as a collective enterprise and view each employee as worthy, capable, and deserving of professional respect and support.

*Next practices* drive people and organizations forward, requiring that a leader know how to identify and constructively challenge their own invisible logics, limiting beliefs, embedded assumptions, and implicit biases since, when unchecked, these constrain the ability to drive authentic workplace reflection, collaboration, and progress. Importantly, next practices challenge people's deficit orientations by repositioning them as limiting logics. Next practices require examination to learn from our default mindsets and behaviors—those that have worked well in the past but keep us stuck in a comfort zone that now limits our growth and progress. To accomplish this, leaders need to engage in productive self-reflection as a key lever of adaptive change.

*Leader reflexivity* is a leader's engagement in active reflection to adjust their thinking and behavior and it grounds and drives leader and organizational adaptability. Leaders who *proactively* create the conditions for employees to reflect, and share ideas, perspectives, and concerns authentically (i.e., without fear of backlash) see exponential relational return on investment for their intentional and active stance of reflection and their highly attuned leadership approach. Building self- and relational trust is essential for work to work into the unknown future. The Flux 5 offers a leader and wider organizational learning framework, a holding environment for inquiry in which to practice new mindsets and skills that help people navigate organizational change that is quickly becoming "less structure, more design."

Agile leaders and organizations move not just with, but ahead of, the times; they demand and evince a receptive sensibility and skillful responsiveness to the competing demands of social and organizational flux. This requires leaders to grow their ethic of relational care, an evergreen task. Leaders need new frames to understand the impacts of this elongated time of flux as well as tools to move their organizations toward a strengthened vision and sense of purpose and workplace belonging. This is generated through focused workplace learning and development processes that foreground people's stories and priorities as catalytic and collaborative professional development.

Learning agility is the goal of mindset work. A leader's *learning agility*—the cognitive and behavioral flexibility developed as an adaptive growth mechanism—helps build a shared sense of purpose and responsibility for current work and future conditions. The canaries in the coal mine of workplace change have signaled that clinging to outdated business approaches and linear modes of workplace interaction results in losses, diminished capacities, and exponentialized opportunity gaps and costs. *Precarity is now endemic to strategy*. The Flux 5 teaches leaders to "honor the space between no longer and not yet" (Levin, 2015) as a foundation for everyone in the organization to do the same.

## Mindsets for Adaptive Change

> Nothing is constant but change! All existence is a perpetual flux of being and becoming! That is the broad lesson of the evolution of the world.
>
> —*Ernst Haeckel*

Adaptability is the single best predictor of organizational success and sustainability of organizational efforts. Effective leaders in today's mercurial workscape are highly adaptive, able to navigate a constantly shifting professional landscape rife with emergent challenges. Harvard leadership gurus Heifetz, Linsky, and Grashow created *adaptive leadership* to advance the understanding that *change, not homeostasis, is the norm in organizations*. This practice-focused framework was designed to help leaders and organizations adapt to changing environments and effectively respond to change. Adaptive change requires new kinds of learning for shared problem definition and solution implementation; it drives organizational response to industry demands, aligns goals and vision with strategy and enactment, and drives solutionary approaches to change in and beyond organizational flux (Heifetz et al., 2009b).

Adaptive leaders engage complex change as it unfolds, enacting shared processes to identify and resolve recurrent organizational challenges; they understand that complex problems are solved most productively with cross-sectional stakeholder input from people across the organization who work most closely to the phenomenon so that It can be viewed through different lenses and angles. Unlike traditional approaches to organizational change, which rely on visioning and problem-solving from top-level leaders, adaptive change integrates a wider and more strategic swath of organizational knowledge and as well mines tacit and siloed organizational knowledge to address challenges in maximally effective ways. As Lao Tzu presciently averred, "When the best leader's work is done the people say: 'We did it ourselves.'"

**Adaptive leadership** supports leaders, teams, and organizations to adapt to complex challenges in rapidly changing environments. It helps organizations adapt and thrive in the face of complex challenges by preparing everyone, as stakeholders, to cultivate self-reflection and cognitive flexibility skills in the process of change. Adaptive leadership involves diagnosing, interrupting, and innovating to build individual and team capabilities that align with and drive organizational goals, values, and vision. Growth occurs when an organization discards ineffective norms and ways of operating. In their place, leaders implement more finely attuned approaches and then monitor their impact with transparency (Heifetz et al., 2009b).

Adaptive leaders foster individual, team, and organizational adaptability, creativity, and innovation through boundary spanning, an approach to cross-function and role integration that enables teams to set course, create alignment, and build shared commitment across horizontal, vertical, stakeholder, demographic, and geographic boundaries. Leaders accomplish boundary spanning through intentional engagement with a range of individuals, groups, and units across the organization, and by pacing learning to create strong flows of information, ideation, and insight generation for organizational development. Adaptive leaders foreground communication and knowledge flow between people from a range of positions, backgrounds, and locations in the organization. This approach is revelatory for leaders and transformative for teams and organizations.

Adaptive leaders proactively build skills to identify, understand, and address root causes of workplace problems, challenges, and bottlenecks. In times of flux, adaptive leaders view and position change as important and useful, discern the benefit-to-risk ratio of specific challenges, and seek out diverse sources of feedback and ideas to seed their choices and decisions; they are ready and able to shift organizational direction, make new decisions, and redirect purpose when necessary. This proactive and responsive approach creates the conditions for catalytic organizational change and enables people to adapt and thrive together (Heifetz et al., 2009b). Heifetz frames six process principles for implementing adaptive organizational change:

1. **Go to the balcony** to get critical distance so that you can reflect, consider, and see the big picture.
2. **Identify adaptive change** proactively and in dialogue with people across the organization. Let inquiry guide the process. Ask many questions.
3. **Regulate distress** so that people are not on edge yet provide enough tension to maintain a shared sense of urgency and challenge unproductive norms.
4. **Maintain disciplined attention.** Identify distractions and stay attuned to complex issues, helping others to do the same. Resist personal, team, and organizational defaults.
5. **Return the work to the people.** Change workflows to elevate accountability and shared responsibility. Instill confidence, encouragement, and support across units, roles, and teams.
6. **Protect the voices below,** of leaders and trailblazers at all levels; support and protect those with the courage to question, speak up, and dissent.

## Adaptive Leader Profile

Adaptive leaders facilitate individual, team, and collective capacity building so that everyone is prepared and able to be adaptive, to collaboratively question the status quo, diagnose problems, develop solutions, and enact change. Adaptive strategies enable teams and organizations to work together to diagnose, interrupt, innovate, and build shared capacity, to solve emergent problems in real time together. Adaptive leadership helps leaders and organizations prioritize collaboration and reject top–down, transactional leadership styles. Adaptive leaders come in all shapes and sizes but share several key characteristics and values, including that they are:

- **Goal-oriented**—motivated to plan, organize, and complete tasks and commitments, they connect change to organizational goals so that actions are guided by specific objectives.
- **Challenge-oriented**—they understand that people's perceptions of challenges are what cause issues and view challenges as opportunities for learning and growth.
- **Open-minded**—they are receptive to new ideas, kinds of knowledge and expertise, and nested perspectives. They actively challenge assumptions, ideas, and beliefs and both value and model a growth mindset and ethic of open-mindedness.
- **Emotionally aware**—they work well with people's emotions (including their own); they value trust and are present, humble, and responsive to the emotional ethos of teams.
- **Committed**—they manage change well, devote time to change efforts, and keep people focused on big-picture goals. They are resilient, persistent, and committed to the work of adaptive change.
- **Proactive**—they are prepared and work to be ever-ahead in challenge identification; they invest organizational resources (including their own time) to diagnose and solve issues.
- **Uncertainty thrivers**—they view and approach uncertainty and problems as resources. They work strategically and collaboratively to develop organizational processes to leverage new situations.
- **Experimental**—they are solutionary, keen to experiment and troubleshoot, listen, reflect, create dynamic flows of ideas, and redirect as needed. They value practice and understand that tackling complex issues requires risk, trust, and collaboration.

Adaptive leaders situate everyone in the organization as problem-solvers who belong inside change processes. As Richie Norton (2013) avers, "Everyone needs to be viewed and treated as a leader, because roles and responsibilities will always be in flux." As the rolling effects of COVID-19 continue to impact organizations and the global economy, adaptive change is especially necessary and relevant.

In an adaptive organization, diverse opinions are valued since every team member is viewed as an adaptive problem-solver. An adaptive leadership approach generates more impactful solutions than traditional approaches can, fostering:

- **Emotional intelligence:** adaptive leaders value emotional intelligence and have high EQs (emotional IQs); they understand and affirm people's emotions generally, and specifically as they 'feel the feels' of change. The ability to be present, to read and respond well to people's emotions, builds trust and helps to create the conditions for solutions to be cultivated in ways that motivate achieving goals collaboratively. Compassion is no longer an add-on for leaders; it is a foundational competency.
- **Organizational equity:** adaptive change requires analyzing organizational policies, formal and informal, to identify and eradicate biases and to create opportunities to hybridize knowledge for improved organizational performance and more equitable outcomes. Leaders committed to equity seek out a diverse range of stakeholder perspectives to challenge the status quo and innovate for organizational equity in policy, process, practice, and professional development. Adaptive leaders and teams are keen to try out new strategies and ideas that prepare the organization for equity-focused change.
- **Growth and development:** adaptive change requires that leaders create the conditions for all employees to grow through processes of shared learning around organizational change. Adaptive leaders value innovation, experience, practice, trying out ideas, and taking creative risks. They commit to everyone's growth in the organization, including themselves as the lead learner.
- **Transparency, character, humility:** adaptive change requires leader and organizational transparency, character, and humility. Adaptive leaders are comfortable owning their mistakes; they model relational openness, self-reflection, compassion, and humility. Adaptive leaders understand the need to change processes and embrace changes that benefit the organization, viewing vision and idea hybridization as vital.
- **Solutionary perspective-taking:** adaptive leaders understand that everyone has a perspective they value and they work to implement win–win solutions through solutionary decision-making approaches. Adaptive leaders examine social and ecological factors to understand how context mediates processes, experiences, and perspectives to develop durable solutions; they do not simply chase what is easy or go for short-term benefits.

Adaptive leaders understand the need to bring the right, if not always the most predictable, people with them into diagnostics and decision-making processes. They share their vision, are open to being questioned and challenged, and, amid the tyranny of the urgent, they model empathy, integrity, grit, and transparency. This creates the conditions for the organization to tap into a broader array of ideas to co-create solutions. Harnessed well, adaptive change promotes individual, team, and systemic sense-making and organizational re-attunement for better overall functioning, as well as to achieve cultural and inclusive excellence.

## Challenges to Adaptive Change

Committing to a process of learning, *and the unlearning that deep learning requires*, helps leaders cultivate increasing openness to transformational learning in times of change and flux. People need to see that it is not just OK for them to be wrong or 'fail' as they take risks to name problems, opportunities, and bottlenecks, but that it is desired. This happens most fluidly when people are encouraged to actively listen and try on new ways of thinking and doing without threat of repercussions.

People tend to resist change in organizations because it feels uncomfortable, and, for some, even existentially threatening (based on past experiences that get triggered, as discussed in Chapter Two). This resistance is not something to judge or resent; rather, it is something to try to understand and redirect, an endemic part of human nature, an extension of our survival instinct gone awry. An adaptive leader strategically invests energy and mobilizes resources across the organization to drive organizational attunement through adaptive change. Adaptive change processes generate new knowledge, ideas, and diagnostics to learn, reflect, and make real-time adjustments. Adaptive change emerges from engaging the collective intelligence of employees across an organization as they learn their way toward solutions together.

Discerning between *technical* and *adaptive challenges* helps teams understand, identify, and strategize adaptive change. *Technical challenges* are clearly understood, with clearly defined solutions; they can be solved through traditional top–down approaches because there are limited and bounded solutions. *Technical* challenges are not the most wicked of organizational problems; they are the more common kind of problems.

| Technical Challenges | Adaptive Challenges |
|---|---|
| • Can be resolved using protocols, <br> • procedures, rules, regulations <br> • Are easy to identify <br> • Are solved by outside experts <br> • Can be fixed with predetermined strategy | • Are resolved through <br> • innovation, discovery, experimentation <br> • Are difficult to identify <br> • Are entrusted to team members <br> • Take time and require thoughtful emergent strategy |
| Technical Solutions | Adaptive Solutions |
| • Are generally received well <br> • Can be executed by decree <br> • Require technical knowledge and facts | • Are generally resisted <br> • Cannot be implemented by decree <br> • Require adaptive collaboration |

*Adaptive* challenges, on the other hand, require emergent learning, solutionary thought partnership, and a strategy reset. *Adaptive challenges* are more complex and unpredictable, requiring coordinated input from multiple people within an organization. Adaptive challenges require contextual understanding to define and learning to build customized solutions.

Understanding these two types of organizational challenges helps leaders and teams understand the kinds of changes they need to prepare for as well as discern when adaptive change is necessary. Addressing adaptive challenges calls on leaders to unlearn a common misperception, to understand that the so-called 'soft skills' are really the 'hard skills'—it takes practice and focus to cultivate emotional and cultural intelligence, for example, which are difficult to develop without adopting an inquiry mindset that enables us to challenge our socialization, conditioning, and the invisible logics they form which shape all we do.

*Resistance to change*, a hydra of many heads, must be addressed proactively, lest it threaten even the most positive workplace change. Adaptive leaders expect employees, stakeholders, and clients to exhibit multiple forms of resistance when change is on the horizon. This gets expressed in the workplace through intentional marginalization, deflection of responsibility and accountability, attacking or maligning others, managing up dishonestly, and toxic interpersonal triangulation. These derailing behaviors surface when employees feel disequilibrated by ensuing (or even possible) organizational change. Only when leaders know to expect these behaviors and negative dynamics can they proactively address them and promote personal reflection, relational accountability, and systemic sense-making.

Fear of dispensability, anxiety about learning new skills or technology, and self-doubt are silent killers of workplace adaptability and progress. Employees across sectors tend to fear change, viewing it as something that threatens their position or status. Thus, consciously or unconsciously, people tend to try to undermine change before it can fully take root. Carol Dweck's (2008) seminal work on growth mindset is about the internal power all people have to reframe challenges, missteps, mistakes, and failures as meaningful, generative opportunities for reflection, learning, and growth. The Flux 5 derives from, as it contributes to, a growth mindset, the mother of all mindsets.

Power + unchecked ego = the greatest challenge to adaptive change. This equation sums up a familiar workplace phenomenon: ways that ego gets acted out, masked, or cloaked in other arguments and behaviors. People's unwillingness to listen and change direction in response to other people's suggestions, opinions, and critiques is a hallmark characteristic of this phenomenon. Adaptive change guides leaders to choose collaboration over enacting or allowing others to enact unilateral power (which is driven by the ego); it requires, as it demands, leader listening, valuing people's ideas and the bravery it requires to share ideas up the power structure, and taking direction from multiple sources of expertise rather than exclusively from traditional or hierarchical ones.

Adaptive leaders work to shift dynamics that limit the flow of ideas to and from a few individuals or units. Employees who are used to having control over decision-making may struggle to relinquish their habituated sense of control when moving to more shared decision-making processes. Leaders must get ahead of and actively address these kinds of ego-based power struggles because they are possible derailers that are proactively addressable. A *distributive wisdom approach* (discussed in this chapter and revisited in the Conclusion) is an organizational approach that maximizes learning through centralizing diverse perspectives and kinds of expertise through processes of knowledge hybridization—a hallmark of adaptive leadership.

## Adaptive Mindsets in Flux

"Pure experience" is the name I gave to the immediate flux of life which furnishes the material to our later reflection with its conceptual categories.

—*William James*

How do being an adaptive leader and the Flux 5 mindsets relate? Workplace research shows that mindset work is the most effective way to create the conditions for people to identify and authentically challenge their own thinking and behavior, individually and on teams. Mindsets govern how people think about the world and ultimately how they fare within it, providing frames for all thinking and behavior. *Organizational mindsets* are how individual mindsets circulate and coalesce in organizations, for better and worse.

Innovation generated through mindset development has the capacity to transform the work environment one person and one team at a time, in a diffusion effect. Cultivating a growth mindset, for example, is vital to developing innovative and resilient employees, teams, and organizations. Innovation requires risk and creativity, and a growth mindset helps people to reframe failure and mistakes as inevitable parts of learning and, even more so, as opportunities for focused growth and learning.

As workplaces face changing workforce demographics and an increasingly ideologically polarized population, leaders face exponentializing challenges that require new skills for effectively addressing these issues along with the tyranny of the urgent. Prioritizing equity and pushing into knowledge siloes are necessary for organizational improvement and success. However, this moment has surfaced as much motivation to drive equity as to push back on it. It does not help that people tend to feel exhausted and traumatized, that the boundaries between work and home, healthy and unhealthy, have become blurred in the third year of a pandemic. Professional development expectations and offerings have changed. Opportunities for natural mentoring have diminished or vanished, given new rhythms. Shifts in how professional learning is (or is not) happening and in its content and quality require recalibration as we watch old mindsets quickly become challenged and outdated.

Leaders build the adaptive change bridge as they cross it. Relational authenticity, self-awareness, and learning agility are necessary to lead in visionary and responsive ways in times of growing need and emergent accountability. Despite the increasing need for such qualities, leaders share that interpersonal awareness, relational authenticity, perspective-taking, and compassion have never felt more elusive in the workplace. Leaders need to create new inroads and systematic processes to prioritize workplace reflection, the development and assessment of emotional and cultural intelligence, relational accountability, and humanization.

The Flux 5 offers a *practice framework* to try out new mindsets as you need them so that you can address the challenges you face with confidence and creativity. This approach helps leaders foreground shared purpose, extend organizational vision, and build relational trust while building forward. The book is designed to be a gateway to building your own learning agility and cognitive flexibility, which adaptive change demands. Adaptive leaders understand it is not just a matter of thinking outside, or even beyond, the box. They know *the box is not even a relevant construct*. Change and innovation happen through seeing beyond the confines of current norms. We circle back to this idea and its implications in the Conclusion.

The Flux 5 is a *leader learning agility framework* comprising five mindsets that help leaders cultivate adaptability and humanize the innovation demanded by today's workplace (see Figure 0.1). Hands-on learning frames and activations illuminate ways these mindsets drive and support adaptive systems. The Flux 5 helps cultivate each mindset as an integrated leadership growth plan. Each mindset has specific and broad applicability for addressing workplace challenges and creating workforce possibilities. As you practice these mindsets, ask yourself: *What kinds of change does today's workplace change make possible?* As you advance organizational purpose or team learning agility, for example, you will see how, through the Flux 5 leader learning ecosystem, cultural and inclusive excellence emerge.

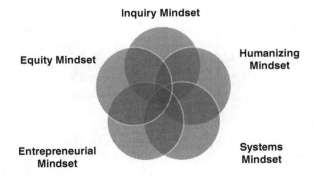

FIGURE 0.1

## The Flux 5 for Adaptive Change

Leaders around the globe and around the corner report the need to take on more emotional and relational dimensions of the workplace. The Flux 5 offers a set of curated practices, learning frames, and activations to help leaders prioritize organizational processes that address emergent issues in ways that foster workplace bravery and inclusive excellence. The first two mindsets, the inquiry mindset and humanizing mindset, are foundational to how organizational learning ecosystems take root in flux. They create the learning ecosystem foundation and mainframe, priming leaders to become increasingly self- and interpersonally aware—both broadly and specifically in terms of workplace equity. The inquiry mindset and humanizing mindset help leaders—ultimately with their teams and across the organization—to challenge unquestioned logics and ask the next set of questions that *disruptive innovation* requires.

The systems mindset and entrepreneurial mindset shape how leaders drive and enact purpose, strategy, and management within systems through human-centered innovation and systemic sense-making. The equity mindset, the fifth mindset of the Flux 5, horizontalizes equity, emotional intelligence (EQ) and cultural intelligence (CQ), racial literacy, and identity-based stress navigation skills across all five mindsets. Self-awareness and interpersonal communicative competence are essential for optimal workplace engagement, experience, and performance. An equity mindset is appreciative and human-centered: it creates the conditions to drive organizational humanization, equity, and cultural and inclusive excellence.

## Leaders as Portals

In her *Financial Times* article "The Pandemic is a Portal," luminary Arundhati Roy (2020) criticizes the Indian government's humanitarian failure to provide equal protection for all its people during the COVID-19 pandemic. Roy contextualizes this pandemic within the long history of global pandemics that have radically altered the world. On this timeline of human suffering and resilience, Roy places COVID-19 as a necessary portal—an opening that we can, and must, widen collectively to enact global political, economic, social, environmental, and spiritual change. Roy inspires us to strategically unlearn and reflexively remake forward:

> Whatever it is, coronavirus has made the mighty kneel and brought the world to a halt like nothing else could. Our minds are still racing back and forth, longing for a return to "normality," trying to stitch our future to our past and refusing to acknowledge the rupture. But the rupture exists. And in the midst of this terrible despair, it offers us a chance to rethink the doomsday machine we have built for ourselves. Nothing could be worse than a return to normality.

Historically, pandemics have forced humans to break with the past and imagine their world anew. This one is no different. It is a portal, a gateway between one world and the next. We can choose to walk through it, dragging the carcasses of our prejudice and hatred, our avarice, our data banks and dead ideas, our dead rivers and smoky skies behind us. Or we can walk through lightly, with little luggage, ready to imagine another world. And ready to fight for it.

Leaders must be agile learners to imagine and build another world in this moment of radical flux. Following the 2008 financial crisis, global business leaders were encouraged to adopt a crisis-as-opportunity strategy—to reimagine work. Reimagining work in this way required, as it now requires, the cultivation of mindsets and approaches that enable leaders to confidently break with the known and established, to enact disruptive innovation. For those of us ready to create new ways of doing work, workforce trends such as Quiet Quitting are a clarion call for change. We must work together to build back not only better, but within, for, and through a new and different paradigm of work. To do so we must work to affirm, converge, and amplify our individual and collective stories, spheres of influence, and wisdoms of practice as we shake the knowledge tree down to its socially reproductive roots. We must collectively work to reimagine and rebuild the world of work.

Evidence shows that mindset work offers the clearest path to sustainable learning for individuals, teams, groups, and organizations. *Mindsets* are established beliefs that shape people's sense-making and influence their behavior and decisions. A leader's mindsets mediate their and everyone else's organizational experience and the felt impact of a crisis or dramatic change in an organization. Leaders *are an environment*, as discussed in Chapter Five. Based on her research on crisis leadership, the Wharton Business School dean, Dr. Erika James, avers,

> Effective leadership is the one factor that creates the potential for an organization to be better off following the crisis than it was before … Crisis leadership is a continuous process that involves developing a mindset for reflecting, adapting and learning from the crisis situation and its aftermath. This requires the ability to strategically scan the environment for knowledge … In a crisis situation, the individual leader's learning should happen in tandem with the organization's learning.
>
> *(James & Wooten, 2011)*

Adaptive leaders need to actively leverage this moment of workplace precarity to build and bridge, reorient and reimagine, and to grow integrated knowledge. Leaders *are portals to new ways of imagining and doing work*, creating organization milieux wherein even the toughest leadership challenges, struggles, and conflicts are leveraged in support of impactful individual and group learning and catalytic organizational change.

*Leader Mindsets for Adaptive Change: The Flux 5* offers a framework for leaders to practice new mindsets, behaviors, and strategies that buoy you, your team, and your organization in today's flux. Leaders are the bridge to new organizational logics, behaviors, processes, and systems that humanize work. *Leaders are portals the moment they decide to be*, embodying the great poet Rumi's words, "Wherever you stand, be the Soul of that place."

## This Book

*Leader Mindsets for Adaptive Change: The Flux 5* was created for you. It is also intended to be read and engaged with by your executive team. Have them read this and engage with the parts you prioritize and what lights different people up. Drive this framework and its practices through teams across the organization as purpose-focused and human-centered professional development that can level the organization up in key performance areas in a changing marketplace. The book offers leaders and teams novel frames and learning activations that help create the ripple effect of adaptive learning and change throughout your organization, starting with you.

The **Introduction: Leader Mindsets for Adaptive Change** frames this moment of flux in the world of work and offers the Flux 5 mindsets as a generative approach to learning and leading organizations in a time of rolling workplace precarity, new kinds of leader and organizational accountability, and complex change. The chapter introduces the Flux 5 framework—inquiry mindset, humanizing mindset, systems mindset, entrepreneurial mindset, and equity mindset—within an adaptive leadership approach to support a visionary and responsive leader, team, and organizational learning ecosystem for these times of organizational flux. The chapter introduces leaders to the flux framework as a bespoke learning ecosystem for cultivating learning agility and skills for a new workplace era, starting with you as the lead learner and then in ever-widening spheres of organizational development. The chapter foregrounds ways that leaders can serve as portals to their own and others' transformational growth and learning at a time when organizations must offer inspiration, humanization, purpose, and equity.

**Chapter One, Inquiry Mindset,** describes an inquiry mindset, which lives at the intersection of critical thinking and disciplined curiosity, helping leaders, teams, and organizations to actively question norms, status quo logics, and organizational defaults through making dominant organizational arrangements problematic. An inquiry mindset evinces constructively critical systemic sensemaking to cultivate organizational self-understanding, enabling leaders and teams to identify and challenge knowledge siloes and invisible logics that block idea hybridization and constrain innovation. An inquiry mindset evinces active learning about self, habits of mind and practice, context, and process understandings; it supports thoughtful and responsive organizational adjustment that considers deep learning activated through self-reflection, relational engagement, training, and professional development. Chapter One offers learning frames and activations for the cultivation of individual, team, and systemic sense-making through an inquiry mindset.

**Chapter Two, Humanizing Mindset,** offers concepts and practices that help leaders drive an organizational culture of humanization and belonging at a time when teams and organizations need both. The chapter describes a humanizing mindset as an antidote to workplace approaches based on Industrial Age values which bred transactional modes of interaction that can be dehumanizing and inequitable, and that have become newly problematic and ineffective. This chapter offers curated workplace learning approaches such as workplace storytelling, story-based inquiry, institutional holding, and inner-resource cultivation skills-building for leaders and teams to move the dial on workplace humanization by cultivating relational trust, and a sense of shared purpose and belonging. It offers rich reflective practices for identifying implicit biases and the invisible logics—yours and those embedded in the structures and habits of the organization—that limit the individual and collective ability to see and interpret the workplace, others, and self clearly.

**Chapter Three, Systems Mindset,** illuminates the value of leader understanding and contextual comprehension and addresses the interconnectedness of cross-organizational system components to effectively communicate and advance organizational purposes and goals. The chapter offers leaders dynamic frameworks for ongoing organizational analysis, synthesis, and emergence, with discrete activities and tools that use feedback loops to prioritize relatedness and transparency. The chapter illuminates the generative value of continuously questioning unchallenged and often invisible organizational logics and assumptions to promote an appreciative decision-making ethos that drives adaptive change while successfully navigating complex, dynamic, emergent challenges.

**Chapter Four, Entrepreneurial Mindset,** outlines the strategic mix of skills and traits that cumulatively grow a leader's ability to recognize and seize opportunities in unpredictable, uncertain, and often ambiguous environments and times. The chapter introduces a reliable and valid instrument designed specifically to measure the entrepreneurial mindset, the Entrepreneurship Mindset Profile (EMP)™, comprising 14 discrete domains, seven skill scales and seven trait scales. The skills and traits include the capacity to generate ideas, execute those ideas, embrace risk, persist through ambiguity, and maintain confidence, which are leveraged through several learning activations: prototyping, goal orientation, market sizing, and pressure testing to help leaders, their teams, and their organizations continuously innovate and adapt.

**Chapter Five, Equity Mindset,** locates equity in the current work and social moment to guide leaders as they work to build an ethos of cultural and inclusive excellence. The chapter offers the equity mindset as a leader and organizational mindset for driving equity, inclusion, and belonging in the workplace.

The chapter addresses current pushback to diversity, equity and inclusion (DEI) initiatives including current models of diversity, equity, and inclusion (DEI) and frames DEI as an adaptive problem to offer new frames for understanding and responding to emergent issues related to workplace equity. The chapter defines concepts and terms that tend to be opaque; it offers specific content knowledge, reflection, and perspective-taking skills, learning activations, and curated insights to help leaders level themselves, their teams, and their organizations up to the state of equity-mindedness and inclusive excellence that employees and clients expect and demand.

The **Conclusion, Leader as "the Space between No Longer and Not Yet,"** returns to the notion of leaders as portals to both specific and broad growth and humanization—their own and that of everyone in their organization. The chapter offers five integrating conceptual frames to catalyze your learning as you carry forward what you have learned into your leadership. The chapter explores the unique remit of leaders in this time of workplace flux and offers concepts useful to bringing this work to life in your leadership, executive team, and across the organization.

# 1

# INQUIRY MINDSET

> The highest activity a human being can attain is learning for understanding, because to understand is to be free.
>
> —*Baruch Spinoza*

## What Is an Inquiry Mindset?

An **inquiry mindset** drives an intentional learning stance on professional practice and the structures and norms shaping that practice. An inquiry mindset shapes leader and organizational values around critical thinking and disciplined curiosity—valuing questions over certainty, practice over automation, collaboration over hierarchy, humanization over hyper-productivity, process along with outcome. Leaders with an inquiry mindset are bullish on uncertainty, thought partnership, and realization before implementation, continually questioning the status quo to improve upon it.

An inquiry mindset enables leaders to be their most intentional and reflective, to ask ever-deeper questions that help them explore a range of perspectives to inform decisions, set strategy, and gather necessary information and data. Leaders with an inquiry mindset see the direct relationship between leader reflection and systemic sense-making; they examine the meaning and outcomes of results, methods, and models from multiple nested perspectives. An inquiry mindset drives disciplined organizational curiosity, active learning, and thought partnership; it supports impactful systemic sense-making for organizational self-understanding.

The flux of current workforce change creates an unprecedented opportunity to transform organizational strategy, norms, behavior, and functioning. A leader's inquiry mindset opens new doors of understanding within process, and in a

DOI: 10.4324/b23253-2

diffusion effect, across the structures and processes of an organization. An inquiry mindset has the potential to recast the workplace as a learning organization that foregrounds a range of perspectives and hybridizes knowledge in ways that make room for dynamic learning and adaptation. An inquiry mindset evinces a leader's commitment to active self-reflection and relational learning in the effort to build knowledge *of* practice, *in* practice, and *for* practice (Cochran-Smith & Lytle, 2009).

It is a game changer when a leader can "make the familiar strange and the strange familiar," meaning they know how to reevaluate and see that which is already familiar to them anew and more critically, and likewise to see that which is as yet unknown to them as more akin than they perhaps first imagined. Seeing things more critically from a distance helps leaders understand *the socially constructed nature of work*. This means that value and meaning, and the logics and processes they generate, were made up to suit the needs of times long past; these ideas were absorbed over generations, unconsciously, through socialization and conditioning within rules generated by the elite. Value and meaning are socially constructed, created from the unconscious agreements people make through social conditioning that imprints beliefs and logics on us that we carry forward as the Truth of ourselves and the universe.

The realization of the socially constructed nature of things is productive for individuals and the workplace—but only once we see and harness it. When identified, this more critical understanding of self and/in society is useful; understanding social constructions illuminates that value and meaning are dynamic rather than static and unchangeable. Understanding this is deeply and widely possibility-inducing. Understanding the values imprinted on us and the invisible logics we carry with us creates room for new ideas and meanings to emerge in the place of habituated thinking patterns.

An inquiry mindset generates understanding that useful knowledge comes from a range of sources rather than exclusively from traditional or expected ones. A leader with an inquiry mindset is authentically curious and shows up as a curious learner, seeking out diverse kinds of knowledge to challenge their own constructed notions of reality, ideas, and value systems. An inquiry mindset helps leaders notice and surface outdated notions of what constitutes valid knowledge and expertise, and of who is a 'knower,' which enables them to identify and challenge a range of limiting beliefs, invisible logics, and unexamined (often unconscious) assumptions that drive workplace decisions, behavior, and dynamics.

An inquiry mindset is embodied in the words of seminal educator-scholar Paulo Freire's words in *Pedagogy of Freedom* (2000):

> Curiosity as restless questioning, as movement toward the revelation of something hidden, as a question verbalized or not, as search for clarity, as a moment of attention, suggestion, and vigilance, constitutes an integral part

of the phenomenon of being alive. There could be no creativity without the curiosity that moves us and sets us patiently impatient before a world that we did not make, to add to it something of our own making.

An inquiry mindset supports, generates, and leverages curiosity and creativity.

## Why Do Leaders and Organizations Need an Inquiry Mindset?

A leader with an inquiry mindset shows up as a curious, reflective, humble, and engaged learner rather than as a knowledge dropper or unilateral expert. This leader questions self and seeks to hybridize ideas, learn from the wisdom of others, and de-silo knowledge. Leaders with an inquiry mindset ask solutionary questions to disrupt useless knowledge silos and champion a *distributive wisdom approach* that enables them to bring diverse perspectives and kinds of expertise into dialogue for continuous learning and improvement.

An inquiry mindset compels leaders to look beyond the binaries that shape and limit organizational thinking; binaries are characterized by an either/or construction, which results in polarized and limiting thinking: an idea is good or bad, a person is Black or White (when many people are mixed race), something is urban or rural. Binaries reduce understanding of lived complexity and are generally inaccurate because they lack nuance. An inquiry mindset evinces the ability to seek out and engage challenging ideas and critiques, which flows from understanding that deep learning requires thought exchange, vulnerability, and constructive critique. Oversimplification does not lead people or organizations anywhere good. An inquiry mindset propels an adaptive relationship to complexity, change, and flux.

An inquiry mindset is a habit of mind, situating oneself as a receptive learner who centralizes shared learning rather than assuming knowledge of everything resides at the top. A leader with an inquiry mindset understands that learning comes from a range of sources and creates openings for formerly hidden or occluded knowledge to emerge in integrated ways. An inquiry mindset is built upon a stance of active questioning and learning, situating expertise in ways that hybridize knowledge and experience through shared questioning, inquiry, discovery, and solution-making.

Cultivating an inquiry mindset enables leaders and teams to create new frames and answers to driving organizational questions, helping organizations to develop the awareness, skills, and differentiated knowledge necessary to recast the organization as a learning environment that, among other things, generates vital place-based or 'local' data about employee perspectives, experiences, ideas, and needs to drive equity and humanization in the workplace. This stakeholder-oriented inquiry process shapes understanding of the need for, and how to drive, adaptive change. Local data, meaning data from the workplace (perhaps related to external metrics), help leaders and teams identify and contextualize patterns to develop more nuanced and customized strategic objectives and processes to evaluate them.

An inquiry mindset generates organizational learning, enabling leaders, teams, and organizations to:

1.   Expand employee mindsets and skill sets
2.   Develop inquiry processes to inform decisions and strategy in real time
3.   Ground decisions, strategy, and processes in local data
4.   Deepen awareness of diverse experiences across roles and units
5.   Enact impactful professional development tailored to workplace needs

Leaders with an inquiry mindset lead from curiosity; they have the will and skills to question and change the rules when they no longer make sense, to reshape the organization to respond to local needs, and to redefine the work people do when internal roles and industry need to shift. Inquiry mindset leaders inquire into, co-create, and elevate a sense of shared purpose and belonging across a relational ecosystem of thought and action partnership. Leaders with an inquiry mindset lead intentional processes of information, data, and perspective sharing that agitate sedimented knowledge silos and loosen knowledge-sharing blockages to create robust knowledge flows.

An important realization generated by today's workplace flux is that some organizational approaches and behaviors no longer serve the same, or even any, purpose. An inquiry mindset illuminates changing realities and needs one thoughtful question at a time, helping leaders 'make the familiar strange,' meaning making the familiar and habitual visible for critical inquiry, and 'make the strange familiar,' meaning seeing the value in ideas generated from different spaces, places, and people as necessarily useful and instructive. An inquiry mindset creates the conditions for leaders and teams to:

1.   Identify implicit biases, assumptions, invisible logics, and norms
2.   Position oneself and show up as a curious and reflective learner
3.   Question organizational knowledge silos and idea marginalization
4.   Identify and engage diverse knowledge, ideas, wisdoms of practice
5.   Champion knowledge sharing and hybridization

An inquiry mindset foregrounds the role of reflection in practice, viewing inquiry as an ethic of daily practice and a fundamental aspect of organizational vision; an inquiry mindset commits leaders and teams to processes of growth and learning through processes of focused self-reflection and systemic sense-making, engaging the organization in thoughtful investigation into, and evidence-based critique of, professional practice and the norms and processes that shape it.

An inquiry mindset invites person-centered, systematic, and proactive approaches to organizational sense-making for cultural and inclusive excellence. Inquiry routines, discussed in this chapter, enable leaders and teams to actively resist confining norms to adeptly address the challenges of organizational life in flux.

## Inquiry Mindset for Adaptive Change

In a time when organizations need new constructs and ideas to drive human-centered innovation beyond old 'thinking outside the box' mentalities (see the Conclusion), an inquiry mindset helps leaders and teams make unconscious thoughts and invisible workplace arrangements conscious and visible, which enables the excavation of limiting beliefs and invisible logics that work against collaboration, progress, relational trust, and equity in organizations. Given the importance of understanding invisible logics to leader mindset and growth work, this section includes a discussion of invisible logics that is followed by learning frames and activations to uncover invisible logics in the tools section of this chapter.

Transcending an Industrial Age worldview wherein dominant organizational design was closed, fragmented, transactional, and extractive means learning to humanize people and create meaning and purpose in the workplace. Adaptive workplaces understand that work needs to be transformational, not transactional, and collaborative, rather than hyper-individualistic and isolating. When the industrialized world operated through a more linear model, ideas lived in black/white binaries, and strategy was the Holy Grail. Now, inquiry is necessary to drive adaptivity in a diffusion effect. Data show that curiosity is a major determinant of leadership acumen when harnessed well. An inquiry mindset is the harness. As Constance Friday notes, "Curiosity did not kill the Cat, it transformed the Cat into a Lion".

Purpose has little value in a milieu where inputs and outputs define people and their value. An inquiry mindset reveals deeper meaning in the seemingly mundane, helping leaders to connect the dots of meaning and purpose through engaging in humble inquiry (Schein, 2013) in ways that reinvigorate individual and shared organizational purpose. Purpose is a core leadership resource as the workplace, and society more broadly, becomes increasingly complex and ambiguous. Most organizations mistakenly position leaders as *the* instrument for maximizing efficiency and output—so much so that it has become an expectation. Volatility, uncertainty, complexity, and ambiguity make this transactional approach to leadership increasingly untenable.

An inquiry mindset helps leaders and teams to see, learn about, and illuminate broader meanings and purposes at play in any organizational context, process, problem, or decision. This informs decision-making and collaboration in transformative ways. An inquiry-based understanding of organizational structure and functioning leads to improved vision and focus. This is no longer an add-on luxury; it is an organizational imperative for survival in a new work order.

New leadership approaches are a necessary response to increased accountability demands, as argued in "Leadership in a (Permanent) Crisis," by Heifetz et al. (2009a) of the Center for Public Leadership at Harvard Kennedy University. As they aver, successful leaders "Foster adaptation, helping people develop the 'next practices' that enable organizations to thrive in a new world, even as they continue with best practices necessary for current success." Developing *next practices* requires cultivating a receptive sensibility grounded in a nuanced and actionable understanding of people's experiences and perspectives across the organization.

Leaders with an inquiry mindset drive workplace inquiry to help the whole organization learn, connect, and build relational trust, as well as to reenergize collaboration and innovation, especially in times of flux. This requires understanding how responses to rapid change are experienced across the organization. As Heifetz et al. (2009a) illuminate:

> The issues themselves are more than disembodied facts and analysis. People's competencies, loyalties, and direct stakes lie behind them … In a period of turmoil, you must look beyond the merits of an issue to understand the interests, fears, aspirations, and loyalties of the factions that have formed around it … [this] requires that you *create a culture of courageous conversations* … Executives need to listen to unfamiliar voices and set the tone for candor and risk taking.

An inquiry mindset helps leaders create the conditions for a culture of courageous conversations, first with themselves through the reflective process of courageous noticing and admitting to self (Edwards, 2015) and then within their spheres of influence across an organization. Courageous conversations require active listening and broad stakeholder engagement and serve to catalyze positive change in teams and organizations. The approach can be integrated into performance appraisals, mentoring and coaching models, team processes, and professional development.

Courageous conversations require, as they generate, openness to individual reflection and relational learning through solutionary and appreciative inquiry into group functioning and communication norms, relational trust, and interpersonal dynamics (see the discussion on brave spaces in Chapter Five). This is supported by an inquiry mindset, which helps leaders to build and hone specific skills, competencies, and organizational conditions of trust and psychological safety. A driving organizational inquiry question is: *How can inquiry become a mindset rather than a series of disconnected projects or events?*

Links between increased individual insight and systemic sense-making, improved productivity, and return on investment provide a strong rationale for institutionalizing workplace inquiry. Positioning inquiry as central professional development exponentializes flows of information, foments collaborative solution development, and pushes disruptive innovation from the inside. The tools section offers hands-on exercises to cultivate an inquiry mindset in ever-widening spheres of influence. Before that, we share one of the most powerful leadership tools available: *invisible logics*.

## Invisible Logics: Leader Superpower or Kryptonite

The word logic originates from the Greek word *logos*, meaning inference or argument. ***Invisible logics*** are tacit lines of reasoning that propel inferences and interpretations and guide habits of mind, frames of thought, and arguments even as they remain invisible. Invisible logics comprise our foundational interpretations about the way the world—and specific phenomena within it—works. Logics form our mental frames for interpreting the world and ourselves. Invisible logics create our purview, delimiting what we can see and what remains beyond the frame, limited by the aperture. Logics are imprinted on us as if they are objective values, whereas they are subjective and socially constructed.

Our logics do not walk around announcing themselves to us, though peers and colleagues farther along in their learning journeys may be able to detect them from our behavior. To us, it is just us, just how we think, the internalized culmination of what we have experienced and what we know from it. Logics are imprinted on us; they shape our view of the world through our formative socialization as we grow up. These logics, shaped by the values, beliefs, and logics of others with influence and power over us (parents, teachers, coaches, role models), are internalized by us as our own. Over time, they become invisible to us, seen as fact, as "the way things are" to the extent that we assume others would have the same reasoning, make the same argument, or come to the same conclusions as us (through a process called projection, discussed in Chapter Two).

Adaptive leaders understand that everyone is conditioned to see the world differently; our unique backgrounds shape how we see, what we see, and how we make sense of it. They work to identify their own invisible logics and see organizational logics as the powerful guides for workplace values and decisions they are, without conscious awareness or explicit discussion. As a thought exercise, observe two people arguing. Watch carefully for how their respective invisible logics guide their behaviors and how this shapes the ways they engage with each other. When observing others through this lens, invisible logics can be clearly discerned. However, our own invisible logics are not clear to us—that is, without conscious reflection and repeated practice. It takes ongoing self-reflection and dialogue to excavate our invisible logics. This is a growth opportunity at scale.

Our invisible logics may be invisible to us, but people around us with more awareness in these areas can discern them from our actions (and inactions). This matters to how leaders understand the limits of their own self-awareness. Just because they cannot see their own driving logics does not mean others do not see them or that they do not notice that leaders themselves are unable to see themselves clearly. Leaders often appear in ways they themselves do not see or comprehend, given how constrained their view is by the aperture of their current logics. A powerful activation tool, SEE, in Chapter Two, helps leaders excavate their invisible logics and scan the work environment to notice others' as well. Invisible logics are different from, though related to, implicit biases, discussed in Chapter Five.

An inquiry mindset, supported by workplace inquiry routines, enables leaders and teams to identify and challenge invisible logics and limiting beliefs and norms through reflective approaches to professional development. Leader learning agility requires lenses and logics to be adjusted with curious humility. Logic scans, a learning activation tool shared in this chapter, help leaders and teams identify hidden logics that shape mindsets and workplace processes. This requires addressing the three Ds—denial, deflection, and defensiveness—through processes of self-reflection and nervous-system management skills development, discussed later in this chapter. As an inquiry process, reflexive scans enlighten the workplace through surfacing hidden logics that have become sedimented into organizational structure, process, norms, and behavior. These scans are done using observational notetaking, alone or in teams; they are a bedrock professional development tool.

## Organizational Inquiry: Local Data Drive Informed Change

Leaders routinely seek out external metrics to make decisions on workforce trends. The Flux 5 offers the approach of rapid-cycle inquiry as a maximally efficient and effective way to strategically scan and understand the environment for knowledge and insights in ways that support adaptive change. Massive workforce, workflow, and workplace shifts require actionable understandings of the myriad contextual changes and challenges currently affecting workforce experiences, processes, and outcomes. Building knowledge of emerging realities with homegrown, quick-cycle data supports leadership that is particularly attuned to micro populations within the workforce, be they based on role, social identity, or affinity.

An inquiry mindset helps leaders attune to the range of diverse perspectives, roles, concerns, ideas, and needs through evidence-based workplace processes. In our work with leaders, we use a discovery framework called rapid-cycle inquiry (RCI). RCI is an efficient and engaging approach to context-informed and human-centered decision-making and strategy. Transcending current workplace challenges—a hydra with many heads—requires thinking beyond the box, not just outside it. The following examples from our work with leaders and teams illuminate how using local data can drive decision-making and adaptive change.

## Example 1: Culture Clash Excavated

A major U.S.-based corporation acquires another large national company. As the acquisition proceeds, pushback from the acquired company impedes the integration process, especially confounding knowledge transfer and communication pathways. The CEO decides to intervene in what was becoming a costly and increasingly hostile chasm between companies.

He designs a quick-cycle investigation of the companies' respective cultures and succeeds in positioning the inquiry's findings to leverage a revised change management plan. Through a rapid 2-week inquiry, a strategically selected sample of executives, middle managers, and front-line employees is interviewed in flash focus groups. Flash focus groups elicit perspectives, concerns, and needs with respect to the short- and long-term future of the newly merged business. An observational component, consisting of walk-throughs focused on corporate culture, was conducted as well.

One discovery was the weight of promises made early on from the top of the house that were not kept. This failure, combined with multiple moves experienced as hostile by employees at the acquired firm (one example was tearing down the old company's sign, which had been there for decades, without asking if they wanted to keep it), created considerable mistrust and intense resistance. However, the flash focus groups generated useful data about employees' concerns along with their clear recommendations for improvement. Selected executives and management were involved in flash data analysis. Results were shared with all employees to open dialogue and demonstrate the company's renewed commitment to transparency and trustworthy communication.

This example shows how even a quick inquiry into corporate culture, structure, and functioning led to improved organizational clarity on how to enact the change management plan. Companies need to function as learning organizations that harness an inquiry mindset to foster learning and development. This is the *raison-d'être* of the lead learner's role.

## Example 2: Applied Research for Action

A chief learning officer (CLO) of a youth marketing firm has grown increasingly concerned about what he worries is a mismatch between the backgrounds of the employees and their clients in terms of age and generational values. He believes their lack of understanding of youth culture impacts the company's ability to provide more resonant and impactful services. His team designed a rapid-cycle inquiry to examine their clients' backgrounds and expectations of marketing services. To conduct this workplace research, an applied research team did the following:

1. **Identified driving questions:** They developed quick-cycle research questions to explore the relationship between client cultures, company culture, and employee demographics. How does culture influence perspectives on services and products? What are the multiple cultures of youth, and how can the company better understand and address them? Since diverse input generates more complex questions and helps build engagement and understanding, they vetted these questions by groups with representation across functions, levels, and social identities.

2. **Reviewed existing knowledge:** The team read about youth culture, subcultures, and the diverse cultures that comprise company employees. A quick review of relevant literature led the research design. This ideally happens before, during, and after data are collected.

3. **Researched design:** The team chose a representative group of youth and employees to question over a 2-week period to generate multiple perspectives on the company's products and services. They aimed for data triangulation with multiple, intersecting data sources to enhance validity and reduce inference. They mapped the timeline.

4. **Collected data:** Data collection methods included existing data from flash focus groups with a subset sample of youth and employees.

5. **Analyzed data:** Once data collection was completed, they analyzed the data together, looking for themes to uncover new understanding.

6. **Reported and shared findings:** The team disseminated findings in a one-page report, organizing the driving issues by considering the data. The report focused on the implications for the company's strategic plan.

Increasing the flow of information and collaborative solution development means pushing innovation from the inside; this happens by engaging employees in the structured pursuit of learning to increase understanding. This requires seeing the value and possibilities for workplace research and understanding that it can be done quickly and well. Leaders must be strategic proponents of workplace research, inviting a range of people into processes of organizational discovery with the potential to reinvigorate the workplace and transform individual and team functioning through impactful professional development.

Leaders can develop researchable questions from workplace concerns that can be answered through rapid-cycle inquiry. Familiarity with workplace research design and understanding how stakeholder involvement is achieved position workplace research as a strong investment. The focal consideration is aligning methods with driving research questions. Leaders we coach seek stronger evidence to guide their decision-making, but often do not know where to begin. Or workplace research seems too complicated, expensive, or time intensive.

Overcoming these common misconceptions of evidence-based decision-making is key to making workplace inquiry a mindset rather than a series of isolated projects. Today's leaders must establish the central role of applied research in organizational learning. As Brené Brown offers, "Stories are data with a soul."

Leadership books written before the pandemic tend to rely on centralized concepts of organizational culture. This requires recalibration, given that foundational structures, norms, processes, and even supply chains have suddenly become outdated, and workplace culture has become rapidly and decidedly decentralized. *Unpredictable, constant change is today's workplace culture.* Embracing cognitive strategies for personal and organizational growth, with the focus on inquiry processes, supports responsive leadership of an adaptive organization. At the very least, it avoids preventable issues and stress. Cultivating an inquiry mindset requires breaking old habits of mind and routines that no longer serve the organization well.

The Flux 5 bridges leader and organizational inquiry and learning, strategy, and adaptive change with workplace equity and inclusion efforts. Each chapter offers a mindset- and skills-building road map with curated activations for learning integration in real time. This helps you to build the bridge of visionary organizational change as you cross it, unwavering in your confidence, avoiding ideological pitfalls, and cultivating a strong and receptive leader stance at a time when it matters more than ever.

## Learning Frames and Activations for an Inquiry Mindset

### Tool 1: "Practice Stopping": Leader Reflection Process

Spiritual leader Thich Nhat Hanh shares, "Many of us have been running all our lives. Practice stopping." Reflection is how we stop, or at least how we slow down for a bit to think. Reflection is a powerful tool for leader learning and cultivating adaptive teams and organizations. Regular self-reflection supports an inquiry mindset and is essential to identifying areas of needed growth to tackle. Through the practice of inquiry-based reflection, leaders develop targeted skills.

It is vital to create *inquiry routines* that drive and support ongoing reflection at the personal, team, and organizational levels. Remember, inquiry and focused self-reflection include thought partnership with others—we all need help to see ourselves accurately, especially when emotions and stakes are high.

Reflective practice can begin with simple questions about an interaction:

1. How did I feel during the interaction?
2. What was I feeling and thinking while it was happening?
3. What were some of the ways I reacted and behaved?
4. What can I learn from how I managed this experience?
5. What will I do differently next time?

Leaders can maximize reflective learning in several ways, including:

1. **Creating inquiry routines** to support consistent reflection amid the tyranny of the urgent. Schedule 10 minutes a day to begin. Proactively block this time to ensure commitment. Extend to 15/20 minutes a day over time if you wish. Ten minutes a day will significantly impact on your leadership.
2. **Writing it down.** Writing offers focused commitment to self-learning. Start by getting a journal or downloading a notetaking app. Write your ideas, emotions, and thoughts from daily experiences. Be as descriptive as possible to deepen your understanding of your emotions and their influence on your thinking and behavior in real time.
3. **Starting with a single focus then expanding.** Focusing on self-reflection may feel overwhelming at first. Focus on a singular event to give yourself the chance to reflect on moments within the event and how they contribute to how things played out.
4. **Practicing honesty with yourself.** Be true to yourself as you reflect on the experience. Acknowledge areas you need to work on and improve upon. Remember, this is to help you grow as a leader. Be honest with yourself.
5. **Adjusting, adjusting, adjusting.** There is no one-size-fits-all approach to reflection. Keep things engaging, test different ideas to find what works. Adjust regularly to strengthen your will to continue engaging in reflective practice. Adjust the amount of time or writing modality. Switch it up so it stays fresh.

The inspiring words of others—writing, poetry, quotes, music—can help keep leaders and teams in the reflection game. As Saint Augustine wrote,

> People travel to wonder at the height of the mountains, at the huge waves of the seas, at the long course of the rivers, at the vast compass of the ocean, at the circular motion of the stars, and yet they pass by themselves without wondering.

Indeed, each of us is a wonder worth traveling within for deep exploration. The depths of learning and growth are endless.

## Tool 2: Create a Space between Stimulus and Response

Jean-Paul Sartre (2003) offers, "What is important is not what happens to us, but how we respond to what happens to us." Creating a space between stimulus and response is a powerful inquiry tool that helps people become their most curious, grounded, and thoughtful. Learning to navigate and manage our own nervous system is where our personal power and an organization's growth's edge reside. The stimulus–response exercise teaches people to create a space of calm, a place of emotional respite to go to and rely upon in even the toughest of moments of conflict and flux.

Through advancing self-reflection that attends to how specific situations arouse emotions because they are wired into our nervous system through conditioning from youth, leaders create the conditions for their organization to develop stress identification and navigation skills writ large. Reflexive self-learning about ways in which thought and response patterns are hard-wired into our nervous systems enables us to develop more authentic communication pathways that help to promote personal agency and organizational trust. This process illuminates that it is not only possible, but expected, that we manage our emotions in the workplace in ways that are healthy for us. This means we need to be given the chance, and the proper scaffolds, to create an internal space of calm for moments of acute tension, distress, and chaos.

Viktor Frankl was an influential social psychologist who spent his life's work—after surviving a concentration camp during the Holocaust—conceptualizing and teaching people about this internal space of calm they can create within themselves. His work offers a path for each of us to cultivate our own safe inner world, even within unsafe or chaotic external realities. Translated from his German writings, Frankl offers this: "Between stimulus and response there is a space. In that space is our power to choose our response. In our response lies our growth and our freedom" (Frankl, 1946, 1977).

Read this line again to take it in: "*Between stimulus and response there is a space. In that space is our power to choose our response. In our response lies our growth and our freedom.*"

This is a liberating insight—that, between what is said or done to us, whatever happens to us, the challenges we face, we can each build our capacity to visualize and enter an inner space of calm intention. This space enables us to freeze our internal clock to calm down our nervous system and gain perspective and clarity before we respond. In our work with leaders and teams, this is a powerful activity for organizational growth. It is a primer for all other professional development, including organizational culture and equity work, since these professional development topics and processes tend to trigger people's histories, which activates their emotions at work, a place not yet set up for reactive emotions.

*Leaders are the primary instrument of workplace learning.* Our work with leaders and organizations begins here, at the root of the root—the human psyche and nervous system. People cannot learn well about anything, and especially about themselves, unless they are able to keep their nervous system calm enough to remain present, curious, open, and compassionate, especially during moments of intense stress and emotion. Leaders can learn to activate this space for themselves, creating a space to visualize between what is said or done and their first

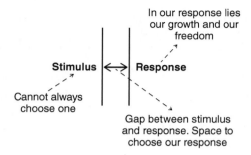

**FIGURE 1.1**

spoken reaction (see Figure 1.1). This space is the crucible of adaptive leadership. Creating this space is teachable; it is an inquiry practice. This practice enables response over reaction, which is a hallmark of cultural and inclusive organizational excellence.

Our work with leaders and organizations undergoing organizational change or in some form of acute or situational crisis shows that it is possible to create an inner space of calm to rely on in times of chaos and flux. Once awareness of the space grows through practice, so does trust in self to *choose* our response to any and all incoming stimuli and situations. Creating and stepping into this inner space awaken the realization that, while we cannot control what happens to us, we can control our responses, which is personal power. Once leaders practice the stimulus–response exercise, they come to trust that they can cultivate this space. They carry it as a portable inner resource, an internal space of calm to count on in moments when calm is externally inaccessible.

The ability to be calm matters a great deal to healthy organizational functioning. When leaders model calm, present, curious professionalism, even when—especially when—they or those around them are negatively emotionally aroused, they give themselves and others not just permission, but enthusiastic invitation and expectation, to engage in workplace inquiry.

Inquiry is an invitation to non-judgmental, disciplined curiosity towards ourselves and others, tensions and disagreements, disruptive learning and innovation. To get there, leaders examine why they interpret, react, and behave as they do, digging ever-more deeply into the *why* of reactions and behaviors to see how these stem from individual socialization and conditioning but can be (mis) understood as neutral and shared (more on this in the discussion of projection in Chapter Two).

The ability to create an inner space between stimulus and response is infinitely liberating. Once you build the space and see the benefits of using it in moments of stress, a new sense of personal agency is born. This is an absolute game changer for leaders and teams. In the space between what happens to and around us and how we choose to respond, leaders create the conditions to notice, consider, and challenge socialized knowledge, cognitive distortions, and implicit biases—to see how habits of mind shape values, expectations, and approaches in the workplace. This process builds self-trust and then, in circles of learning, group trust, which is even more essential in these trying times (and forever more).

## Stimulus–Response Mindfulness Exercise

Psychological safety is a primary criterion for building effective teams, yet it is difficult to create a sense of safety when we feel stuck in a fight or flight mode. This exercise teaches people to tend to their central nervous systems as the first step in working to build psychological safety within themself, teams, and the organization. Humans are animals with a prefrontal cortex; this exercise breaks down the physiological stress cycle to teach people to notice and harness their biology to their benefit.

1.  **Choose a stressful work situation:** ideally, this is a recent work experience that surfaces a present tension or conflict that you feel with some charge. It can also be an old experience that still revs you up because it was never resolved. The charge is the point.
2.  **Write to center the event** in a quick free-write with no grammar rules. Jot down context cues, memories, and feelings attached to the memories. Writing offers the mind focus that directs it to new layers of situations.
3.  **Briefly tell the story** of this event to your partner; attend to major aspects of the experience and how it made you feel over the arc of the event. As you do:
    a.  **Be curious about yourself** rather than judgmental. People tend to judge themselves and assign value to things rather than taking an inquiry mindset to consider the socially constructed nature of value. Instead, you can observe yourself in a more detached and curious way, meaning without ego investment and conditioned thought processes to generate self-learning and development.
    b.  **Visualize a space** between a specific stimulus (what is said or done to you) and your response to it (how you react)—imagine a calm and quiet space. Picture the space in your mind's eye—a peaceful place, a place you step into consciously with the intention to identify your emotions when things feel overwhelming.
    c.  **Use breathing to slow down your thoughts** so that you can fully notice and inquire into them. Breathe deeply in and out several times, slowly, staying conscious of the pace of your breath, the weight of your chest, and how it feels in your body when your breath slows down and settles. Stay with your breath as often as you can, especially in times of tension and conflict.

d. **Notice your self-talk.** What do you say to yourself without noticing it on a typical morning? When you think you've messed up? What do you notice yourself saying in your head about yourself to yourself about this situation or event? Are there patterns in what you message to yourself about this that are old? That are no longer useful to you? Some that are even harmful once you notice them? Notice specific words and phrases you say to yourself and consider their origin and meaning, the power they hold over you—is your inner voice critical? Would you speak to someone you love and respect this way? Consider the sources of your self-talk; recall how it was shaped.

e. **Reflect on where this self-talk comes from.** How old are the phrases you say to yourself when you mess up? Whose voice/s do you hear—a parent or other person who shaped your sense of self? When do you first remember hearing this voice or these messages? What does this help you see about how old your self-talk is, about how it was formed and imprinted on you for lifelong use? Assess if and how these messages are useful and/or harmful to you. Most often our self-talk is harsh because we have taken on the judgments and issues of others as our own. We can shed these old voices to gain inner freedom. Sometimes people are hesitant to rid themselves of negative talk because they think the negative messages are motivating, but psychological research shows that they are not; only positive self-talk is motivating. To think negative self-talk is motivating is a cognitive distortion—a lie we tell ourselves that keeps us attached to harmful behaviors and patterns that we no longer need.

f. **Slow down and reflect on your reactions.** Notice your emotional and physical reactions to this stress and conflict as they happen. Notice how your body feels. Pause. Breathe slowly and deeply multiple times. Assess: *how does my body feel? What do my physical reactions tell me about how I'm feeling right now?* Use the physical reactions as data about what is going on inside you and be curious where they come from—since they are hardwired, they require effort to detect and take in. Consider new ways to react that are more self-supporting and productive.

4. **Strategize** how you will build this inner space for the next time something begins to hook your nervous system. Prepared responses build a stronger sense of personal agency that serves us well in the present.

5. **Pull the lesson out** for your learning and growth and *move on.* When people draw out the lesson, they do not need to keep returning to the same scenario to continue to judge themselves or others over and over, as humans are sadly wont to do. When we pull the lesson out, there is no need for the cycle of negative self-judgment. This is an activated growth mindset.

6. **Find a trusted thought partner** who engages in their own growth work and professional development to discuss how to integrate these ideas into daily leadership and organizational practice. Pick a specific scenario to begin.

7.  **Practice** in small ways every day. Track your progress, take time to reflect, write notes if useful, and debrief with trusted peers as often as possible.
8.  **Discuss steps to inner resolve.** Notice and name what anticipatory concerns present during this conversation: what riles you up? Discuss how *you want to feel* going forward in this kind of situation or others that may present.
9.  **Breathe in and out** slowly several times. Notice your breath and exhale any tension; try to release any negative energy or stress.
10. **Good job.** Pick a different situation and go through the process again.

## Tool 3: Invisible Logic Scans

Workplaces are collection sites of all kinds of bias. Our biases are deeply rooted, structural, and integrated into everything in the workplace: they underlay actions between peers, how work is assigned, how people are disciplined (or not). These issues are structural, rooted in intergenerational habits of mind and the workplace structures, policies, and processes they have generated and continue to uphold. Importantly for growth work, bias is not automatic; it is conditioned over time. However, without conscious awareness and addressing them, biases become implicit and automatic. Biases are possible to change through impactful equity-focused professional development and accountability structures.

Take a moment of pause. As Franz Kafka (1996) observed, "Association with human beings lures one into self-observation". Invite yourself to engage in challenging self-reflection. Remember that deep work is discomforting more than gratifying. Seek out a trusted peer or mentor who will challenge your thinking (and their own). High-quality peer mentoring relationships stretch leader capacity.

### Five Scans to Identify and Process Invisible Logics

Invisible logic scans can be used anytime, anywhere, with anyone. Start by choosing one scan and taking observational notes during meetings or professional development sessions to identify tacit beliefs and invisible logics—your own and others'. These scans are useful within teams and groups for seeing and making connections between individual interpretations and organizational sense-making.

1.  **Invisible logics scan:** Invisible logics are habits of mind and frames of thinking that remain invisible to us—individual and broader organizational logics that guide our values and decisions, often without our conscious awareness. To activate this scan, engage in self-guided inquiry in which you ask yourself: What invisible logics shape my leadership style? This team? The organization? How were these invisible logics formed? What purpose did they serve? Do they still serve that purpose? Which logics shape how

people interact with each other? In what ways? Which logics are spoken, and which are unspoken? Are these logics shared across group members? If not, what does this signal? What shapes these invisible logics? Are they useful to progress or holding them/me/us back? In what ways? Which logics are more dominant? Respected? Deferred to? How does this relate to identity and proximal power? Examine how these logics guide your own and others' behavior and how they are expressed as facts, assumptions, implicit biases, or privileged entitlements.

2. **Emotional labor scan:** *Emotional labor* is a term created by British sociologist Arlie Hochschild (1983) to name the emergent behavioral phenomenon when women went into the workforce in droves in the 1980s across the United States and Europe. The term provides language for the internal experiences of women who found themselves exhausted from working to suppress their emotions and hold back their authentic selves in the face of male-dominated workplace norms and expectations. Emotional labor can also mean feeling compelled to protect the feelings of people with more power while having to explain experiences of racism and/or sexism and endure microaggressions. Emotional labor tends to create cycles of inauthenticity, exhaustion, and resentment. The theory speaks to non-dominant identity groups being judged by dominant group standards, which creates the need to conform, be inauthentic, and perform emotional labor. Emotional labor is a helpful concept for leaders and teams because it illuminates how workplaces are socially constructed and designed to the benefit of those with proximal power.

   The emotional labor scan provides a process for examining this phenomenon with focus on the emotional labor of those around you that may be invisible to you and your own emotional labor, if you feel you engage in it (if not, that is useful information as well). To activate this scan, engage in self-guided inquiry and ask yourself: *Do I see signs of emotional labor in myself? In others? What are they, and how do I understand them? Do I cause emotional labor demands from anyone around me? If so, who? In what ways? Do I create the conditions where others withhold their authentic reactions and ideas (if so, how?)? Do I notice patterns about emotional labor around me? In me? How can I better situate myself to understand the impact of emotional labor on myself and those around me?*

3. **Espoused theory versus theory-in-use scan:** Healthy organizational dynamics and functioning require values alignment between organizational values and objectives for professional growth. Organizational dynamics, circumscribed by power dynamics, require serious attention. Harvard Business School professors Chris Argyris and Donald Schön (1978) offer the concept of espoused theory versus theory-in-use to describe the chasm between theories of action that are espoused in an organization, as in those that are consciously claimed and articulated, and what is enacted in daily practice in systems, as in what *actually goes on* in the daily functioning of organizations. This is central to processes of systemic sense-making.

*Espoused theory* is the values and logics people *believe* drive their behavior. *Theory-in-use* is the worldview and values implied by people's behavior, the maps they use to act. People are unaware that their theories-in-use are often inconsistent with their espoused theories and are often unaware of their theories-in-use in the first place. This framework helps organizations flag mismatches between what they claim is happening and what is actually happening inside organizations and teams. This helps organizations to assess underlying beliefs that guide decisions and actions, which can run counter to what the organization and its leaders espouse to be the values and mission. This theory illuminates gaps between theory and practice.

In this scan, look for evidence of if and how values, mission, purpose, and practice align (or not). This can be on a team, with an individual, or in a broader group. To explore alignment between espoused theory and theory-in-use, examine how a theory of action or mission is present (or not) in behavior; view ways that stated values are met in meetings (or not); and examine espoused values around diversity, equity, and inclusion, for example, to see if and how these are met in daily workplace functioning. *Is there (mis)alignment between the organization's stated ideals and its programs, resources, or daily functioning? If so, what forms does this take? Where and when does misalignment present, and how it is viewed?* Use this scan to identify what is working well in terms of values–actions alignment and what needs to be adjusted to achieve greater values clarification and alignment.

4. **Deflection scan:** Intention is a distraction of the ego. Please reread that. Consider specific aspects of your communication and interaction style that can benefit from reflection and honest examination (for example, reflect on whether, in conversations about difficult topics, you tend to use support-responses or shift-responses and why). Examine your recent and long-standing conflict patterns to gain insight into how others may perceive you. As you do this, consider that understanding has to do less with what is said or intended than with how the words are experienced, the impact that they have. The most effective leaders immediately work to understand their impact and step into their accountability, period, regardless of intention or what the other person did that was worse.

   The healthiest reaction when confronted with our own mistakes or missteps is to stop, reflect on the situation, and step into accountability, no matter what the other person did, said, or made us feel. This can be difficult and uncomfortable; thus, some people choose instead to shift focus or blame away from themselves. In psychology, this is called deflection, and it is one of the most common defense mechanisms when confronted with mistakes or during conflict. Deflecting is a psychological defense mechanism used to avoid accountability by trying to take blame off ourselves. This can happen through passing blame onto someone or something else in a process often called flipping the script. This strategy is largely unsuccessful and creates added layers of unnecessary conflict, yet people are generally not taught that taking blame is a positive, agency-building experience when people have the skills to do it well. These behaviors are a result of people's formative experiences and the specific coping mechanisms they generated when young and getting in trouble or having their deepest inner needs ignored or unmet; these experiences became imprinted on them and indexed as rules to live by. This precipitates an unconscious underlying lack of trust in self and of the understanding that being wrong is okay because humans are always on the way, always becoming, always growing.

The good news is that the maladaptive coping strategy of deflection can be interrupted by engaging in self-guided inquiry. Begin by asking yourself: *When confronted with conflict, do I deflect, feel shame, resist hearing truths that threaten my sense of self? Where do these feelings come from—who taught me to have a negative relationship with being wrong? Does it serve me and/or is it a conditioned reaction? Do I feel more entitled to personal comfort than others around me (why/ not?)? In which kinds of conflicts or confrontations do I deflect, and why? What does it look like when I see others deflect? What is it like when people step into their personal accountability? What was it like when I have? What can it teach me, and how can I learn to do it better over time?*

5.  **Societal trope scan:** A trope is a common convention used often enough to be easily recognized, a commonplace, recognizable plot element, theme, or visual cue that conveys specific meaning. Tropes pop up repeatedly in film, television, and social media—types of characters, settings, plot lines. People internalize these societal tropes, and they become imprinted in our minds as the reality of the world. They can even serve as rationales to delegitimize real people, reducing them to caricatures.

    To activate this scan, engage in self-guided inquiry in which you ask yourself: *Do I notice societal tropes or caricatures of people by social identity group (for example, 'the whiny millennial' or 'the angry Black woman' or 'the emotional woman')? How do these stereotypes make people feel in real time? What impacts do they have on a team or group? How do I make sense of these dynamics as they play out in real time? How do I show up in these dynamics? When am I reducing the people around me to tropes—in conflict, for example?*

## Scan Notetaking Process

The scan notetaking process is vital to this learning activation; it helps us to focus and record as we engage in sense-making. This can be introduced in teams or done individually and shared back into a large group. Scans can be discussed over time as ongoing professional development and discovery. When leaders and teams engage with the logic scans and notetaking process, it tends to get adopted at scale because it is portable, powerful, and extremely cost-efficient (it is free). These reflexive scan processes prompt leaders and everyone in organizations to notice, surface, and consider internalized beliefs and implicit biases that quietly permeate the workplace. It is a win–win–win.

## For More on Invisible Logics

To examine the *formation* of invisible logics, we suggest Ruiz's (2001) *The Four Agreements*, which explores socialization into constraining belief systems. Ruiz offers:

1. **The rules and values of society are imposed on us** through socialization into systems of punishment and reward. We learn to be what others think we 'should' be, come to believe it is not okay to be who we are, and begin to pretend to be who we are not. This is the birth of shame and inauthenticity.
2. **We learn to judge ourselves** according to agreements we never consciously chose. This creates a cycle of self-limiting beliefs based on logics, expectations, and norms that condition us to think this is 'just the way it is.'
3. **The socially constructed framework of our world is handed down to us.** As children, we learned how to behave, what is acceptable and not, what to believe, what is right and wrong, through values transmission that conditioned us unconsciously.
4. **This values and belief system is imprinted on us,** and we use it to judge and criticize ourselves and others, imposing subjective values as objective and creating human hierarchies. This diminishes our personal power.

Personal freedom lives in the ability to identify and change the agreements we made before we had the chance to understand and consciously agree to them. Four new agreements enable us to chart a path of authenticity and personal power:

1. **Be impeccable with your word.** Be truthful, state what you need, say things to have a positive influence. We act on what we tell ourselves is real.
2. **Do not take anything personally.** How others treat us is about them. Not taking anything personally respects people's subjective realities, realizing that their views do not necessarily see or describe us accurately.
3. **Do not make assumptions.** An assumption about what other people think or feel about us is a limiting thought. We cannot mindread, and so we need to seek out evidence before concluding what someone is thinking.
4. **Always do your best.** When we commit to always doing our best, we avoid criticism from our internal judge. Realizing that your best varies over time enables you to replace your inner judge with personal freedom.

The *four agreements* are a leader favorite; they illuminate how an inquiry mindset can drive and support new ways of seeing, understanding, and doing life.

## Tool 4: Workplace Inquiry Groups: Purpose Inquiry Reboot

Inquiry groups are increasingly being used for professional, learning, and organizational strategy because they have been proven effective for sustaining meaningful changes in organizational practice and policy. Inquiry groups come in all shapes and sizes. A leader can structure their executive team as an inquiry group to examine a specific topic during strategically selected meetings. Or they can be formed outside a leader's time with a tight feedback mechanism. Workplace inquiry groups meet regularly to reflect on progress and analyze data, create action plans to improve effectiveness, and develop action plans. Inquiry groups, sometimes called communities of practice, are positioned as part of a larger inquiry system. As Hosea Ballou offers, "Doubt is the incentive to truth and inquiry leads the way".

Workplace inquiry groups decenter codified expertise and seed disruptive innovation. Inquiry groups help to extend the power of leaders by filling in knowledge that leaders may otherwise not be privy to. The approach is collaborative thought partnership wherein everyone on a team brings their own wisdom of practice. Workplace inquiry groups engage with timely issues through quick cycles of inquiry; they can be stand-alone or integrated into team processes and professional development. The goal is to engage in generative, collaborative discovery that addresses pressing issues. Inquiry groups can take many forms, meet on different cycles, and advance a range of goals; they:

1. Share view collaboration as integral to professional excellence
2. Convene work towards a shared interest and goal set
3. Involve members in continuous learning and shared participation
4. Share ongoing dialogic engagement and thought partnership
5. Share collaborative norm building, active listening, and support

Through inquiry processes, new knowledge is created to address each challenge at hand. Inquiry is an organic, intentional, and systematic process; it is flexible and adaptable as data are collected, analyzed, and applied to action, resolving each challenge at hand. Throughout the process, team members document the process, including new and iterating questions, new ideas, and analyses of data. Members share during and after the inquiry, welcoming critique. Depending on context, the results may uncover additional challenges that require further inquiry.

### Purpose Inquiry Processes

An organization's purpose is its reason to exist. Purpose humanizes the workplace and directs the meaning of people's work; it drives and answers the question, *Why is the work I/we do important?* Many organizations need a clarity reboot on their purpose. Inquiry into purpose inspires and motivates, illuminating how employees contribute to purpose through their work.

Purpose inquiry processes take teams through three sequential steps that help them cultivate a shared sense of purpose: (1.) purpose inquiry, (2.) institutionalizing purpose, and (3.) messaging purpose.

1. **Purpose inquiry:** Purpose inquiry is a step-by-step team inquiry process focused on meaningful shared goals. Most organizations lack a sense of purpose or have long forgotten it, so that it needs excavation. To excavate, people share stories, perspectives, and ideas that reveal embedded purpose. This requires a relational approach, listening to what people think and feel; it is inductive and emergent.

   *Stories of organizational purpose*: Leaders use inquiry processes to surface and build stories of organizational purpose through sharing practice-based stories that examine the ways that people explore, experience, and apply purpose in their work in real time. These inquiries work to achieve strategic dialogue that develops a clear understanding of purpose and people's roles in relation to it.

2. **Purpose institutionalization:** Institutionalizing purpose is what drives shared purpose on teams and across the organization. To institutionalize purpose, teams socialize and cultivate organizational purpose through the processes of purpose inquiry.

   *Purpose sharing* is when teams share perspectives on purpose and map purpose onto organizational structures, processes, and policies together. Purpose sharing drives inquiry, providing an integrating principle that enables leaders and teams to balance urgent demands with a longer-term perspective on the purpose, meaning, and health of the ecosystem. Purpose sharing helps to offset reactive mindsets and behaviors through supporting shared inquiry and group reflection.

3. **Purpose messaging:** Purpose is an organization's reason for being, characterized by its significance, aspiration, direction, motivation, and relationality. Purpose must be personalized through intentional organizational inquiry processes. Inquiry questions include: *How do we embed purpose into everyone's role and remit? How do we engage in more humanizing conversations? How do we keep energy and focus?* Dissemination matters in terms of inward and outward messaging that illuminates the meaning and complexity of purpose.

### Tool 5: Rapid-Cycle Inquiry and Applied Research Teams

New accountability in a state of perpetual flux requires adaptive change. Today's leaders cannot simply facilitate adaptation; they must *be* adaptation, leading next practices through societal flux and organizational precarity. This demands a leader's receptive sensibility be grounded in a meaningful understanding of perspectives across the organization, which requires local data production from internal stakeholders. As Marcel Proust wrote, "The only real voyage consists not of seeking new landscapes, but in having new eyes; in seeing the universe through the eyes of another, one hundred others—in seeing the hundred universes that each of them sees" (Proust & Milly, 2003). Strategic perspective-taking to listen and learn about the hundred universes each person sees is the goal and remit of rapid-cycle inquiry.

Rapid-cycle inquiry leverages workplace stories as data to inform real-time decision-making; it surfaces issues and ideas that tend to get backgrounded in times of rapid change. Rapid-cycle inquiry acknowledges the organizational reality that time is the biggest constraint of flux and enables leaders to efficiently consider decisions with strategic input from *across levels, roles, and identities within and beyond precarious moments.* Rapid-cycle inquiry creates opportunities to invite courageous conversations. These conversations offer support and connection sparking collaborative and entrepreneurial thinking—encouraging exploration of new ideas, methods, and processes in an adaptive learning environment.

## Rapid-Cycle Inquiry Methods

1. **Pulse surveys:** brief surveys or open-ended questionnaires
2. **Listening and discovery sessions:** flash interviews, focus groups, listening tours, observations
3. **Multimodal data elicitation:** social media, testimonials, app-based inquiry tools
4. **Participatory methods:** priority and issue mapping, data visualization
5. **Existing data/documents:** prior surveys, minutes, strategic plans
6. **Analysis and discussion:** multi-stakeholder inquiry processes
7. **Inquiry groups/advisory groups:** can be activated quickly when questions, perceived problems, or need for analysis arise.

## Rapid-Cycle Inquiry Template

1. *Who can do rapid-cycle inquiry?* Rapid-cycle inquiry is for leaders, teams, and organizations. This *real-time inquiry method* supports cultivation of organizational learning and humanizing processes. Anyone can engage in these processes. Equitable representation is foregrounded.
2. *What constitutes data?* Traditional modes of research can limit application of real-time data in decisions. Rapid-cycle inquiry makes this possible; it

creates the conditions to gather data from stories in ways that can inform decisions, strategy, and practice. There are many possible data sources in rapid-cycle inquiry. Since workplace data are contextual—that is, embedded within the setting in ways that shape them—stories become the primary form of data. As a first step, ask: *What processes and experiences generate data useful to rapid-cycle learning processes? What narratives can inform existing or external data trends?*

3. *What does the RCI process look like?* This template is used to map the rapid-cycle inquiry process. In the second category below, data collection, choose among these possible data sources based on goals, resources, and contextual factors. It is not necessary or even advisable to do them all; choose those most generative to the focus at hand.

I. **Rapid-cycle inquiry design**
   1. Goals
   2. Issue addressing (i.e., context and action questions)
   3. Existing knowledge, rapid-cycle literature review (e.g., Google Scholar)
   4. Equitable representation (i.e., identities, roles, experiences, perspectives)

II. **Rapid-cycle data collection options**
   1. Rapid-cycle interviews and focus groups
   2. Story-based inquiry
   3. Observational fieldnotes
   4. Rapid-cycle surveys
   5. Rapid-cycle multimodal data (priority/issue mapping/ranking)
   6. Existing data (e.g., documents, social media, internal/external metrics)

III. **Rapid-cycle data analysis options**
   1. Rapid-cycle member checks (data validity)
   2. Rapid-cycle data reads
   3. Rapid-cycle data visualization
   4. Rapid-cycle thematic analysis and discovery
   5. Rapid-cycle meaning-making session(s)

IV. **Rapid-cycle knowledge sharing and dissemination options**
   1. Rapid-cycle discovery debriefs
   2. Rapid-cycle dissemination (e.g., newsletters, town halls, briefs)
   3. Rapid-cycle stakeholder engagement
   4. Rapid-cycle feedback loops (i.e., stakeholder groups)

Using a customized selection of these processes, leaders and teams cultivate an active growth orientation to contextual learning. Rapid-cycle inquiry enables powerful emergent learning and systemic sense-making to be applied in real time.

## Applied Research Teams

Applied research teams are groups of colleagues working together to address a relevant issue or topic. They likely have differing priorities and experiences, and, to be successful, individuals on the team should share a clear, common goal. Most teams working in organizations are unclear about their team's purpose, goals, and rationale. Furthermore, other common-sense understandings about what makes a team successful, including considerations regarding size, goals, skills, approach, and accountability, are often not put into practice. There are not uniform answers to these considerations.

*Who should be on a workplace research team?* This question depends on many factors, including organizational culture and dynamics, human resources and schedules, and the focus of the research. This includes paying attention to social and group identities of team members. If you are examining diversity, equity, and inclusion processes, individuals with different experiences with and understandings of race, racial identity, racial literacy, and racial unease are needed on your team.

Forming a research team involves careful considerations of who should be on the team and how these individuals will interact together and making sure that your research team represents multiple perspectives. Table 1.1 presents questions to help guide the formation of workplace research teams.

**TABLE 1.1** Considerations for Forming a Workplace Research Team

**Topical Considerations**
1. What is the problem/topic we are studying and why?
2. What are the different perspectives we should include on the team?
3. Who should be on the research team? What perspectives do they represent?

**Organizational Factors**
1. What resistance might there be to this topic or process?
2. Whose voices are influential in the organization, and in what ways?
3. Should some of these people be on the team? Why or why not?

**Basic Considerations**
1. What is an ideal size for the team, and why?
2. Is there a dedicated time that everyone can meet? When, and for how long? If not, how and when will the team meet?
3. Does anyone have knowledge of applied research methods?

**Skills**
1. What skills do team members need (e.g., research or facilitation skills, ability to foster effective team dynamics)?
2. What focused skills development is needed at the outset? How will this work?
3. Are there other skills that would be of use?

## Leading Applied Research Teams

For applied research team success, leaders must proactively consider and address team dynamics through building an understanding of team goals, roles, and norms.

## Team Goals

Developing shared goals, roles, and norms is central to effective teams. A key step is for the team members to collaboratively define the goals of their work together to develop a shared vision for their applied research. There are many perspectives, backgrounds, and experiences on every team, and everyone has a different understanding of why the research is important.

Developing a shared goal or set of goals for the team is crucial to ensuring the team is aligned in its work. To develop goals, team members need to learn about each other's visions and beliefs and consider together what unifies their collective work. This does not mean individuals change their personal goals; it means the team is aligned in what it seeks to accomplish. Through the process of determining shared goals, team members gain understanding of each other's perspectives. Once collaborative goals and vision are developed, team members revisit and check in on progress toward team goals.

## Team Roles

Roles refer to formal and informal aspects of how a team is run. Having clear roles entails that team members are aware of their responsibilities. Many of you have probably been on a team in which it is unclear who is responsible for what. A common consequence is that one individual ends up over-functioning because of fear that the job will not get done otherwise. This is antithetical to authentic collaboration, which is what generates trust and durability of ideas.

Specific roles for each team member should be clearly delineated. Roles evolve once a research design is developed. However, there are other factors related to the running of the team and team meetings that can be developed before a research plan has been developed. These are related to the functioning of the team, including who will lead the team meetings, and who will develop the agenda. Will these roles rotate, will the same person always be responsible for these tasks, or will tasks rotate between different members? In addition to having a leader for each meeting, another important role to designate is the 'check-in' leader who ensures that everyone is aligned in goals, roles, and norms as a priority.

## Team Norms

Norms exist on teams whether they are established or not. When norms are not collaboratively discussed and agreed upon, problematic norms develop.

If there is not a shared understanding of how to address conflict on teams, individuals may deal with disagreement in unproductive ways. If there is not a norm for how group discussions are led, the most outspoken team members tend to dominate conversations. Another example relates to the use of computers and phones during meetings. It is quite common for individuals to have laptops or phones out during meetings, even though they are distracting. It is important to the productivity and collegiality of teams that such topics are proactively addressed. Collaboratively considering norms regarding how the team will function is vital to leading effective teams, especially when conflicts or challenges arise. Group norms are discussed in more depth in Chapter Five.

Adaptive leaders proactively address challenges in group dynamics by keeping a finger on the pulse of teams and groups across the organization. They regularly talk with team members to check that the shared commitment to team goals, roles, and norms remains strong and to discuss changes necessary for group functioning and success. This ideally happens in the group, so that discussion and negotiation are transparent and shared within the group.

While there are times to check in with individuals outside group time, being judicious and intentional is important. Encourage direct and clear communication to avoid triangulation (when one member of the group receives a message indirectly from another member in a way that occludes and causes confusion and mistrust). Having norms for feedback and communication should be established and modeled by the lead learner (see Chapter Five).

Table 1.2 presents potential topics for teams to discuss related to developing, establishing, and maintaining healthy and productive team norms.

Figure 1.2 presents professional development activations generated by applied research.

**TABLE 1.2** Planning Questions: Applied Research Team Members

1. How long and how often will meetings be?
2. How will meetings be structured?
3. What is expected of team members during meetings?
4. What work will happen between meetings? How is work shared? How do people ask for help or share questions as they do their tasks?
5. What participation norms are there (e.g., raising hands, jumping in)?
6. How can the group best elicit a diverse range of perspectives?
7. How are decisions made (e.g., by consensus, majority vote)?
8. How do social identities influence interpretations of group dynamics?
9. How will conflict be viewed and addressed?
10. What other principles guide your work together?

*Professional Development Activations Generated by Applied Research*

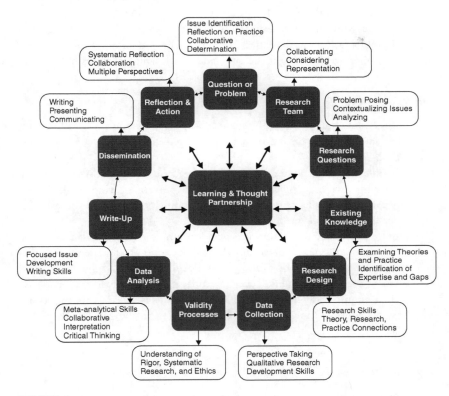

**FIGURE 1.2**

## Inquiry Mindset Practices

Below are several ways to integrate an inquiry mindset into your daily leadership practice. To begin, take the first step today.

### *Try Today*

1.  Choose a morning mantra to seed focus and curiosity (e.g., "I will be curious in my team meeting this morning" or "I will notice new things about ordinary things today").
2.  Identify an inquiry thought partner, a weekly accountabilibuddy. Decide on the first two dates/times. Make this brief (30 minutes) and stick to the time, making sure both people get to share equally.

3. Buy and read a copy of *The Four Agreements* by Ruiz. This little book captures much of what we mean by invisible logics, socialized assumptions, and implicit biases. Discuss with a peer for maximum impact.
4. Structure your executive team as an inquiry group. Select a pressing issue and build a quick and delimited inquiry process into existing meetings.
5. Remember that learning is the goal, and that learning requires unlearning.

## Build a Weekly Practice

1. Engage in a quick morning reflection just before grabbing your phone and set an intention for the day. *What do I want to see or do anew today? What would I like to learn today?*
2. Schedule weekly dialogue sessions with an accountabilibuddy for backstage processing (explored in Chapter Five) and peer mentoring. Pick specific topics or create what is referred to as an inquiry flow where you ask each other questions to keep the ideation going.
3. Think of/use specific inquiry prompts to train your mind to actively question norms and view typical knowledge siloes and arrangements as potentially limiting and worthy of inquiry and deliberation.
4. Write in an inquiry notebook every Monday morning or Friday afternoon to keep an inquiry flow going (or any day that works well to sustain the effort).
5. Acknowledge and reward yourself for engaging in the hard work of self-reflection.

## Try Monthly

1. Attend to your inquiry-based growth with tenacity. To support this, build and support an inquiry team around you for learning and knowledge exchange.
2. Share your inquiry mindset widely to elevate intentional inquiry in meetings. Model it. For example, create new meeting norms for asking questions that get underneath logics and purpose.
3. Drive an inquiry mindset through inquiry groups and applied research teams that explore layered workplace questions (i.e., local data generation).
4. To expand on data and knowledge production from these teams, lead meetings with big-picture inquiry questions for systemic sense-making— proposed by leaders and team members—for everyone to discuss. Effective inquiry building includes questions that evince dialogue about the kind of organizational ethos people want to create in the future. As team members provide input, expand feedback and responsiveness to lift wisdom and generate shared commitment which emerges from co-creation.
5. On the first day of every month, ask yourself: *What is my inquiry for this month?*

# 2
# HUMANIZING MINDSET

My lifetime listens to yours.

—*Muriel Rukeyser*

## What Is a Humanizing Mindset?

A **humanizing mindset** enables leaders to foreground people, purpose, and presence; to promote trust, psychological safety, and shared belonging. Leaders with a humanizing mindset establish a culture of care and interdependence in their organizations through modeling compassion, presence, and appreciative listening. Humanizing leaders work to understand people's complex needs within the organization and remake organizational processes in response to systemic barriers. A humanizing mindset evinces commitment to everyone's optimal development, enabling people to appreciate themselves and each other, build supportive rituals into the workday, and develop self-awareness and stress-navigation skills. To care for employees, humanizing leaders humanize themselves by attending to their own development and self-care.

Leaders with a humanizing mindset see the generative value in scaffolding teams as they learn to skillfully traverse complexity, change, and crisis. They believe that everyone in the organization should engage in professional development to build (and refine) the skills they need to achieve inner calm in conflict and flux. This reflects an abundance leadership approach, which views people and groups through a resource rather than deficit lens. Adaptive organizations work from abundance not scarcity logics; they see and promote an abundance of learning and growth opportunities rather than making them something precious to be competed for in ways that can create toxic dynamics and inequitable work environments.

DOI: 10.4324/b23253-3

A leader with a humanizing mindset is solutionary and caring, promoting cultural and inclusive excellence and relational accountability at scale. A humanizing mindset aligns with and catalyzes Heifetz, Linsky, and Grashow's seminal theory of adaptive leadership (2009b), which illuminates the ways that complex organizational problems require nuanced approaches that help leaders and teams to identify and address root causes of challenges in contextually responsive and human-centered ways. Adaptive leaders are both knowledgeable and nimble enough to identify and address the needs of the moment while adapting the organization for the future.

Dehumanization is a product of Industrial Age-turned-mainstream leadership and management thinking, approaches, and practices (Pak & Ravitch, 2021). As visionary thinker Albert Einstein (1946) presciently observed,

> The world we have created is a product of our thinking; it cannot be changed without changing our thinking. If we want to change the world, we have to change our thinking … no problem can be solved from the same consciousness that created it. We must learn to see the world anew.

The takeaway from this is a seemingly simple yet difficult human act: Change your thinking, change the world.

Leaders and organizations need to rethink their practices, and the logics that promote and rationalize them, to drive adaptive change. At a fundamental level, changing means humanizing organizations to break cycles of structural disadvantage, bias, and exclusion. Adaptive leaders change the rules, reshape the organization, and redefine the work people do in dialogue with a range of stakeholders; they humanize work by creating intentional spaces and processes for shared knowledge generation that disrupt knowledge silos, fostering idea hybridization through a diffusion of innovations approach (Rogers, 2003).

A humanizing mindset enables leaders to:

1. Foreground people, purpose, and presence
2. Promote relational trust, empathy, and belonging
3. Engage in self-reflection, organizational inquiry, and systemic sense-making
4. Build psychological safety, relational trust, and accountability
5. Foreground diverse knowledge, ideas, and experiences
6. Build awareness of shared humanity, interdependence, and shared purpose
7. Cultivate presence and institutional and interpersonal holding skills

These roles, as expectations, have been placed on today's leaders without announcement. Leaders need to understand how to authentically connect with employees to ensure that they (remember that, within "they," there exist diverse sub-groups) feel seen and heard and to offer substantive supports based on what they share. This is an ethic of leader compassion evinced by Muriel Rukeyser's (1968) words "My lifetime listens to yours".

Importantly, listening to another's lifetime requires gaining critical distance from our own; this requires that we take the time to consider the embedded layers of meaning in people's histories and the experiences they carry into their present-day interactions and performance. It means learning to deal with our own projections and how they lead us to assume. It is vital that leaders understand that what they hear is mediated by social identities which are intersectional, meaning everyone has multiple identity markers that live at the intersections of gender, race, social class/caste, and other aspects of identity that create people's relationships to structural and organizational power, privilege, and (dis)advantage. This helps leaders think more complexly about identity and equity, the heart of humanization.

## Humanizing Mindsets to Build Relational Trust

**Relational trust** is the environmental condition that results from how colleagues interpret, perceive, and believe each other's intentions, behavior, reliability, and motives. Relational trust is built through day-to-day exchanges; it evinces the shared imperative to take on the challenging work of adaptive change. Relational trust fosters the organizational conditions for individuals to initiate and sustain activities that are necessary for productivity improvements (Bryk & Schneider, 2002). Building relational trust includes ensuring accountability for shared standards while fostering autonomy and mutual support.

Relational trust facilitates a sense of psychological safety which is vital for adaptive change. To feel psychological safety in the workplace, employees must feel included, safe to learn, contribute, and challenge norms without fear of being embarrassed, marginalized, or punished (Clark, 2020). Psychological safety evinces environments that nurture trust, shared support, and mutual respect. Psychological safety is required for workplace humanization.

Charles Feltman (Feltman et al., 2009), guru of workplace trust, defines trust in a straightforward way we have successfully used with teams to build specific areas of communication and trust. Feltman avers that trust exists when someone makes something important to them vulnerable to the will or actions of another person. Distrust, then, is when someone has shared something important that is not safe with that person.

Building on Feltman's definition of workplace trust, Brené Brown (2019) offers the acronym BRAVING to break trust into its component parts as a way for people to more specifically ask for what they need since the term trust is too broad and weighted down by value judgment. Brown offers trust as *braving* connection with others. The acronym illuminates the component parts of trust:

- **Boundaries** in psychology connote the conceptual limit between two people. Boundaries mean that individuals know where they end and another person begins, what is theirs and what is not; it means acknowledging that every adult is responsible for themself. It means, "I trust you if you are clear about your boundaries, you hold to them, and you are clear about my boundaries and respect them."

- **Reliability** means I can only trust you if you do what you say you will do repeatedly over time. This entails being clear on our limitations to ensure we do not overpromise and can deliver on our commitments, only taking on what we can realistically accomplish.

- **Accountability** means I trust you if, when you make a mistake, you own it, apologize for it, and make amends for it. It is equally true that when I make a mistake, I proactively own it, apologize for it, and make amends.

- **Vault** means that what I share with you is held in confidence and vice versa. It also means that I see you acknowledge confidentiality by not sharing other people's private things. You respect my story and other people's stories.

- **Integrity** means that you act from a place of integrity and encourage me to do the same. It means choosing courage over comfort, what is right over what is fun, fast, or convenient, practicing, not simply professing, your values.

- **Non-judgmental** means I can struggle and ask for help without being judged. When value is assigned to needing help, when I think less of myself for needing help, then, when I offer someone else help, by logical extension I will likely think less of them as well. We need to learn to resist judging ourselves and others for needing help. Real trust only exists if help is reciprocal and non-judgmental—including with ourselves.

- **Generosity** means assuming the most generous thing about my words, intentions, and behaviors and checking in with me and holding me accountable if I miss something, hurt, or offend you.

**BRAVING**, according to Brown, means working to see ourselves and each other as whole, trying, and fallible all at the same time—the human condition. Discerning layers of trust enable more clarity in thinking and communication, illuminating what Brown refers to as "the third story"—the gap between perception and experience that constitutes a third story that lives between people's perspectives.

Storying these gaps is the goal of a humanizing mindset—replacing generalities, assumptions, and distances with the real and authentic aspects of who people are and how they show up at work, individually and relationally (Ravitch & Kannan, 2022). This is the hallmark of workplace learning, which happens through professional development focused on self-reflection and systemic sensemaking for action. Today's leaders must ask not what their organizations can do for them, but what they can do to humanize their organizations. The axiom of work has changed.

## Why Do Leaders and Organizations Need a Humanizing Mindset?

Diminished opportunities for team building in remote and hybrid work have meant the fading of regular hallway conversations and other kinds of informal exchanges and rituals that foster workplace trust and belonging. *What will take its place?* The growing understanding of these workforce realities creates new expectations, needs, relational flows, and stressors that require balance in the professional, psychological, and emotional dimensions of work. It also creates new layers of possibility.

Moreover, the pandemic has evinced pervasive trauma, loss, grief, and distrust between people, leaders, and information. Sweeping responses to racial injustice in the United States and across many countries have crossed sectors, highlighting social polarization, hardening values divisions, and social resentments and creating new kinds of skill mismatches. Most people do not have the skills to deal constructively with these intense macro sociopolitical realities and how they are instantiated in the micro contexts of work such as in the life of teams. Leaders must light the path from transactional to transformational engagement.

It is widely known in employment research that members of non-dominant identity groups experience persistent workplace bias that negatively impacts their professional experiences and trajectories. Biases are embedded in routine organizational practices such as hiring, role allocation, compensation, and promotion. Workplace biases present through microaggressions, structures and processes of exclusion, and systematic underrepresentation of non-dominant groups in top leadership positions.

For everyone, **implicit biases**—biases we carry that we cannot access consciously—stifle our learning and growth. Implicit biases (sometimes called unconscious biases) are attitudes, prejudices, and judgments we unconsciously hold about other people and groups. By definition (i.e., implicit), people are unaware of or unable to pinpoint where the biases come from. Everyone has implicit biases; they are ingrained in our subconscious through our individual experiences, socialization, and backgrounds. For example, people often have biases related to racial groups, including our own. People generally have biases based on race, gender, sexual orientation, social class/caste, and education level, to name only a few.

Creating the conditions for employees to explore their biased thinking and authentically share their perspectives and questions as they reflect on their biases and consider each other's concerns, when done well, promotes transformational organizational learning and health. Leaders with a humanizing mindset bring people together for meaningful professional development, understanding that vision, purpose, and belonging emerge through intentional dialogue, shared questioning, and active listening. A humanizing leader mediates workplace precarity through evoking a shared sense of responsibility for the future.

Shared engagement in systemic sense-making supports a humanizing organizational culture that motivates relational skills development so that employees are better able to traverse complex processes, build trust, and enact cognitive and relational flexibility.

In a humanizing workplace, the knowledge and growth of all members have value and create opportunity. This requires leaders to build a receptive sensibility for communication and conflict so that communication is maximally effective (e.g., communication strategies for sudden plan changes given a collective state of feeling overwhelmed). The ability to engage and gauge emotion with focused compassion supports leaders and organizations to be their most creative, focused, and resilient. Leaders with a humanizing mindset understand that meaningful learning and growth happen through intentional dialogue that productively challenges organizational norms and defaults through inquiry.

A leader with a humanizing mindset understands that communication, experience, and interaction are subjective (meaning that each person interprets things differently), contextual (meaning respective to our individual experiences, past and present), and full of unexamined assumptions (meaning we are the fish in the water of our own assumptions).

A leader's humanizing mindset illuminates how experiences and interactions constitute actionable real-time data—when viewed with intention and curiosity—that can be used to better understand the relational and organizational dynamics of which they are part. Leaders with a humanizing mindset understand that thriving is interdependent and work to:

1. Develop reflection skills for themselves and those they lead
2. Cultivate a critically receptive sensibility
3. Sustain and inspire motivation to learn and grow through challenge
4. Embed authentic knowledge sharing and organizational feedback loops
5. Navigate identity-related stress well and provide structures for all to do so

Communication is vital to organizational humanization; it has the power to teach people to understand themselves and others more fully. It can also shut down learning and silence people. Clear communication norms create a workplace in which a range of perspectives and leaders are empowered to excel (see Chapter Five). Organizational opacity and lack of clarity lead to fear and mistrust. Authentic engagement and belonging are built on transparency and trust. Leading with transparency means expectations are set, aligned, and fulfilled, with feedback loops. Humanizing leader communication leads to greater employee trust in their manager and the organization. Communication needs to feel humanizing, which requires intention, listening, strategy, and care.

Based on her work on workplace equity, change management, and leadership development, Shaista Khilji (2020) frames *organizational humanization* in six interrelated steps:

- **Introspecting** is structured and unstructured inward exploration of *what the organization is and stands for* vis-à-vis identity, mission, and value proposition; it is learning about values and norms that undergird organizational identity and systems.

- **Espousing** is what happens once an organization examines its identity and systems and is ready to redefine itself through a process of imagining an aspirational future state; it allows organizations to establish guideposts for future direction and goals. *Who do we want to become?*

- **Strategizing** is mapping a course of specific actions with a focus on people and business. This resists the organizational default of overlooking or downplaying the human aspects of strategy. To humanize organizations, these human aspects must drive value and receive foregrounded attention.

- **Changing** is the crucible of making adaptive change happen. Organizations must implement processes that meaningfully impact people and policies, evincing the humanizing drive to generate humanizing outcomes for all.

- **Internalizing** is making change the steady state, incorporated into individual and organizational values and norms through behavior and boundary spanning. A humanizing mindset is only possible when daily behaviors and values reflect humanizing principles.

- **Growing** is building in dynamic and rapidly changing environments; humanization requires commitment to continuous learning and improvement. Ongoing reflection, evaluation, and modification of norms, processes, and behaviors are necessary as change evinces new knowledge and insights.

A leader's approach to workplace humanization levels up organizational ability to cultivate relational trust and a sense of shared purpose through processes that foreground vulnerability, compassion, active listening, and presence through organizational processes called *institutional holding*.

## Institutional Holding: More than a Metaphor

*Institutional holding* is a generative frame for understanding the role of leader care and scaffolding in creating organizational purpose, authentic engagement, and belonging, especially in times of challenge and change. Psychoanalytic research conducted by Donald Winnicott, an influential British psychoanalyst, suggests that, when children are consistently held well—that is, with focused attention, care, and balanced concern from their primary caregivers, especially when they are scared or when they feel threatened or vulnerable—they become grounded in a healthy sense of self that enables them to internalize the ability to be resilient and hopeful, even in the face of adversity. The opposite is also true, as Winnicott (1960) states, "Tell me what you fear, and I will tell you what has happened to you."

Winnicott's research on holding environments explored those environments that most encouraged children to make sense of themselves and/in the world with wonder, curiosity, grit, and resilience. He found that caregivers who were emotionally present and available but not imposing or demanding, reassuring but not intrusive or doting, responsive but not reactive, provided a *holding environment* that created the conditions for their children to cultivate their own meaning-making skills to navigate their inner worlds and the outer world, to develop a strong sense of self and the skills necessary to discern their own abilities and limitations, face and overcome hardships, and remain hopeful (Petriglieri, 2020).

Leaders with a humanizing mindset understand that *adults need holding too*—as they face difficult situations and adapt to change. A leader with a humanizing mindset intentionally creates a holding environment for difficult situations, learning, and emotions in the workplace—in teams specifically—and models compassion through demonstrating highly focused attention, care, and concern in spaces that have not always welcomed care or relational engagement in this way.

Gianpiero Petriglieri, Associate Professor of Organizational Behavior at INSEAD, expands the concept of institutional holding based on Winnicott's seminal work. Leaders enact **institutional holding** by strengthening the structure and ethos of a team and the broader organization. Examples include implementing policies and procedures that reassure people about organizational fairness and that promote systems of dialogue and equitable participation in decision-making in ways that enable them to adapt to challenges together, rather than fomenting (or supporting) polarizing factions. Holding describes how authority figures *contain* and *interpret* the meaning of events in times of uncertainty and change. Containing is how leaders alleviate people's distress and support them in making sense of challenging situations with clear-headedness, reassurance, and a clear understanding of purpose, which orients and connects them.

Humanizing leaders promote systems of dialogue that engage multiple perspectives and participation styles to ensure that holding comes from diverse sources—meaning peer-to-peer, not just top–down—and that equity is horizontalized since identities and histories influence how people interpret the world and each other. Institutional holding helps people feel supported even when circumstances are increasingly demanding, and conflicts arise. It is proactive, foundation-building work, a leader's gift to their organization (Ravitch & Kannan, 2022).

Importantly, failing to provide holding makes organizational expressions of compassion and understanding land as hollow. As Petriglieri (2020) states,

> Holding is a more obscure and seldom celebrated facet of leadership than vision, but no less important. And when crises hit, it becomes essential. In groups whose leaders can hold, mutual support abounds, work continues, and a new vision eventually emerges. When leaders cannot hold, and we can't hold each other, anxiety, anger, and fragmentation ensue.

The leader is the guide and the ballast of adaptive change.

There is a distinction between institutional holding and **interpersonal holding**, which is when leaders offer institutional holding through modeling it interpersonally. This requires a leader's present-mindedness over a future orientation, which can be an organizational default in moments of stress. To enact interpersonal holding, leaders bear witness and show compassionate understanding toward people's experiences and concerns, even when there is no clear resolve. Presence and compassionate engagement are hallmarks of interpersonal holding, which gives people permission to feel and attend to their emotions with curiosity and to consider different perspectives in ways that affirm, build personal power, and foster a sense of connection. When people feel helpless, leaders need to create the conditions for them to feel agentic through expressing their experiences, ideas, and concerns.

A humanizing mindset places unique emphasis on institutional holding as central to building a shared sense of purpose, relational trust, connection, and care in the rolling now. A leader's desire and ability to enact *institutional and interpersonal holding* strengthen the entire organization through developing new awareness and processes that build individual and group adaptivity. In a time of heightened fear and loss, budget cuts, and shifts between hybrid and remote work, people need reassurance, transparency, and psychological safety.

Leaders with a humanizing mindset hold people with care and create professional development processes for authentic dialogue and meaningful exchange. They are transparent and compassionate while answering questions and addressing concerns, even when the news is stressful, unclear, or confusing in the moment. George Colman states, "Praise the bridge that carried you over." Leaders are the bridge to more humanizing work experiences and futures.

## Workplace Storytelling

*Storytelling* is a pillar of family, culture, faith, and most societies. Stories are how humans understand the world. Stories hold power to constrain, liberate, create, teach, heal, and transform. Storytelling is a foundational building block of psychology and counseling, the cornerstone of education and schooling, and the heart of many cultures, religions, and communities. Stories shape learning, people's sense of self and what is possible. Stories convey the real and the imagined, sometimes merging them to illuminate a path to the future (Stevenson, 2014). There is transcendent power in stories and in learning how people have been storied—and how we can re-story ourselves and the world around us as a form of *learning into* who we are still becoming. As theologian Rachel Held Evans (2018) wrote, "We live inside an unfinished story."

Storytelling is a powerful approach to team communication and an effective way to improve workplace trust, communication, and belonging. Often, organizations do not know what to do with stories because they are not set up for them yet. People do not often share their stories authentically because it feels unsafe to do so, given workplace politics, bias, and the wider structural discrimination these reflect. When people do share, their stories are often not met with affirmation, understanding, or empathy (Ravitch & Kannan, 2022).

There is transformative possibility in workplace storytelling, in storying and re-storying our experiences, in building counter-narratives to grand narratives that 'deficitize' and dehumanize. The possibility lies in how stories help people to express and listen to experience, to imagine and create. Stories help us connect to ourselves and each other. Storytelling holds transformative promise for adaptive and responsive workplaces.

Stories and storytelling help groups engage in inquiry, reflection, and meaning-making—portals into people's meaning-making processes and the experiences and perspectives of others. Storytelling is increasingly used to center marginalized communities' wisdoms, to affirm and contest false narratives of history, and foment critical awareness (Khalifa, 2018). Marginalization means placing identity groups outside the norms of the dominant culture in ways that devalue their norms and values and even pathologize them as deviant or regressive.

**Workplace storytelling** is a generative approach to story-based professional learning that provides powerful opportunities for identity expression, affirmation, and preservation. Across approaches to workplace storytelling is the desire for growth, resiliency, self-learning, relational learning, and world-learning. Stories are a portal into resonant inquiry, insight generation, knowledge production, identity affirmation, and the cultivation of agentic change—personal, group, organizational—into ever-widening spheres of learning and connection.

Stories illuminate how the personal is political (Hanisch, 1970) and help to dismantle deficit thinking, including the ways individuals take this in/on themselves and project it onto other people and groups (Valencia, 2010). Stories, across time and place, can be positioned and leveraged as vital information for 'undoctrination' from socialized knowledge hierarchies and invisible logics that constrain individual and collective possibility (Ravitch, 2020).

Workplace storytelling is an intentional approach to cultivating intra- and interpersonal awareness and compassion, learning about our storied lives in relation to the experiences and stories of our interlocutors. Intentional storytelling processes—which include a range of approaches for sharing and listening to individual and group stories—help us make deeper and wider (i.e., more critical) sense of our lives, the rootedness of our ideologies and beliefs, and the historical and contextual moorings of our current emotions, beliefs, priorities, and stances. Storytelling helps us examine our invisible logics and belief systems and the broader social, cultural, political, and structural forces that shape them.

Workplace storytelling offers a means of learning and contesting reality, building and preserving teams, conveying knowledge, values, beliefs, and emotions; it allows people to engage in grounded and contextualized self-reflection and to become constructively critical of self *and* society and self *in* society. As Salman Rushdie (1991) offers,

> Those who do not have power over the story that dominates their lives—the power to retell it, rethink it, deconstruct it, joke about it, and change it as times change—truly are powerless, because they cannot think new thoughts.

Workplace storytelling processes teach people to identify, reflect on, and examine their experiences, histories, and values as they explore and challenge the meaning and validity of the information they have and reflect on assumptions, actions, and inactions to identify root motivations and contextual mediators (Khalifa, 2018).

Workplace storytelling processes help people examine how context and history inform thought and behavior patterns, both visible and tacit, in the workplace. It is a powerful tool for learning because the process of telling stories in intentional, reflexive, and relational ways helps people co-create the conditions to identify and consider their own ways of being and, over time, to make sense of the familial, social, cultural, educational, and ideological contexts that shape the ways they interpret themselves and their experiences in the world. This includes ways they have internalized and taken on other people's projections and value hierarchies as if they are the truth of them, making them their own story of self.

In her Ted Talk *The Danger of a Single Story* (2009), Chimamanda Ngozi Adichie speaks to the importance and power of stories for breaking the exclusive hold dominant narratives have on many of our understandings of the world. She says, "Many stories matter. Stories have been used to dispossess and to malign. But stories can also be used to empower, and to humanize. Stories can break the dignity of a people. But stories can also repair that broken dignity." Stories help people to learn, connect, and build relational trust in teams, groups, and organizations. Stories are openings for shared inquiry, understanding, and discovery; for them to be such, leaders must understand their power and learn to use them wisely.

As discussed in Tool 2 below, people's emotions shape their thoughts; they are fodder for limiting thoughts and cognitive distortions that, when identified and challenged, can be processed to healthy resolution. Such limiting thoughts cause internal and relational misattunements that can be shifted to create more liberating possibilities. This happens by changing people's thought patterns in ways that allow them to reimagine themselves and others anew. Storytelling is a dynamic strategy for empowering people to understand and embody an organization's core values. Leaders at all levels can learn how to use storytelling to educate, inform, motivate, and inspire. Stories impart organizational purpose and values as well as individual meaning and values.

## Storytelling Fosters Relational Trust

Workplace storytelling leads to improved trust and connection. Storytelling affects how humans take in information and develop connection and relational trust. *Relational trust* is the sum of myriad interpretations, the collection of interpretations by members of an organization of other members' trustworthiness. These interpretations include perceptions of other members' intentions, behavior, and motives. Relational trust results from members' interpretations, perceptions, and beliefs about other members; it is the sum of individual members' beliefs about other members in a team or organization.

- **Fact 1:** Telling stories activates the neural coupling function of our brain. This enables us to relate what another is saying to our own lives, making communication both personal and relatable. It creates a mirroring pattern in our brains to allow each other to experience similar brain activity.
- **Fact 2:** Sharing stories stirs emotions in the listener, which releases dopamine. This stimulates memory, making what is shared more memorable for longer.
- **Fact 3:** Listening to stories releases oxytocin in the brain. This creates a sense of safety and trust that connects the listener to the storyteller.

## Storytelling Foments Psychological Safety

**Psychological safety** is a state of enacting the authentic self without fear of negative consequences to self-image, professional status, or career trajectory. Psychological safety is the belief that a team, group, or organization is a safe setting for people to engage in interpersonal courage, authenticity, accountability, individual bravery, and risk-taking. In teams that are psychologically safe, members feel affirmed, accepted, and respected. Clark (2020) shares that to feel psychological safety in the workplace employees need to feel included and safe to learn, contribute, and challenge norms without fear of being embarrassed, marginalized, or punished. Psychological safety creates environments that nurture relational trust, shared support, and mutual respect. Humanization requires psychological safety.

## Storytelling Inspires Positive Emotion

Emotions influence decision-making. Every day, employees face a range of decisions, many of which happen behind the scenes on a kind of autopilot. Stirring emotions through storytelling helps teams move into more catalytic and impactful decision-making. As workplace communication, stories humanize and connect people; they evoke positive emotions such as pride and happiness, which brings teams together and builds trust. Storytelling drives people's positive emotions to the benefit of the team and organization.

## Storytelling Cuts through the Noise

We live in a world of constant noise from email, social media, news, and advertisements that bombard us with information. Workplace communication forms part of this cacophony. Tell stories that make your ideas sticky rather than filling employee inboxes with things that get lost in the noise. Storytelling cuts through the noise by evoking emotion that creates empathy. The messages you share through stories are personal and thus more relatable, and so they capture people's attention and become memorable more readily. Leaders use storytelling to ensure that their messages stand out and are remembered.

## Storytelling Creates Growth Opportunities

As you share stories, people are more likely to connect with your goals and messages. Stories are easier to recall, and thus the information they contain has higher rates of response and implementation. Storytelling encourages peer mentoring and sharing information that supports individuals and teams. Sharing data-driven information in traditional ways can lose your audience, whereas storytelling makes information dynamic and easier to listen to, increasing the likelihood of take-up and momentum. Storytelling exponentializes possibility in workplace communication, helping to build an organizational ethos wherein people engage in growth opportunities and enact effective communication.

## Learning Frames and Activations for a Humanizing Mindset

### Tool 1: Story-Based Inquiry: A Workplace Storytelling Communication Tool

**Story-based inquiry** is a semi-structured storytelling process that helps people examine how context informs thought and behavior in ways both visible and tacit in the daily life of work. Story-based inquiry creates possibilities for building individual and group authenticity, resiliency, and learning, helping leaders, teams, and organizations cultivate trust. Humanizing leaders use storytelling to increase connection and deepen learning.

Adrienne Maree Brown (2017) offers the insight that "We are socialized to see what is wrong, missing, off, to tear down the ideas of others and uplift our own. To a certain degree, our entire future may depend on learning to listen, listen without assumptions or defenses." Story-based inquiry builds connection, conveying diverse knowledge, values, and beliefs and exploring their value and productive intersections; it allows people to engage in transformational workplace self-reflection and relationship building.

Through intentional workplace storytelling, leaders uplift a range of experiences and perspectives. Storytelling can be positioned as a portal to insight, knowledge integration, and identity affirmation. Story-based inquiry helps create the conditions for deep listening and constructive perspective-taking in organizations. It helps people understand that assumptions and defense mechanisms are human and dynamic and, most importantly, that they are changeable with practice.

Human beings *are always on the way*—in a process of *becoming*. Given that people's authentic stories are often not viewed as valuable data in the life of organizations, story-based inquiry offers a powerful approach to "storying the gaps" (Ravitch & Kannan, 2022) before they become opportunity costs or more significant problems. Stories are how people share who they are most authentically. With skill, they are a portal to group trust and engagement. These processes are useful when teams need to strengthen sense of purpose and belonging. What follows is an example of a story-based inquiry process from our work in the corporate world.

## Sample Story-Based Inquiry Process

**Topic:** Communication and support issues post-pandemic

**Inquiry:** How has the pandemic affected communication within my/our spheres of influence and engagement?

**Goals:** Set clear goals for inquiry processes so stories are focused and generative. Set times and stick to them. Examples of goals include that sessions will help to:

1. Illuminate specific and broad post-pandemic workforce challenges as they relate to team and manager communication.
2. Create a forum for people to express communication challenges they face in the pandemic as a collective (rather than as individuals; strength in numbers and hive mind).
3. Create shared awareness of issues by putting issues on manager and supervisor dashboards in active and skills-building ways that inform supports, processes, policies, and performance appraisals.
4. Build follow-on supports such as communications tools and professional development plans.
5. Strengthen the sense of connection, trust, and belonging.

## Process and Steps

- First, the inquiry question is stated: *How has the pandemic affected communication within my/our spheres of influence and engagement?*
- Everyone is instructed to choose a personal story that feels emblematic of what communication currently feels like at work.
- Each person is asked to do a 1–2-minute free-write to center themselves in their story (this can be on a laptop, paper, or notes on a phone). The story

can be specifically about workplace moments or something they relate to work to make a point about a current workplace situation.
- Stories are shared after approximately 1 minute.
- Remind people that to achieve psychological safety, which is vital to trust and belonging, people must feel that their confidentiality is honored.

## Round 1

In fishbowl style (people in the center of the activity, with onlookers in clear view around them to take perspective from various angles), key leaders and their teams share their stories and then discuss the communication challenges they face. Story sharing happens one person at a time. Each person has 1 minute and times themself (on their phone or a stopwatch provided to them). A notetaker is assigned. Onlookers are asked to look for and then summarize themes (which can then be matched to the notes for triangulation later if useful).

## Round 2

Breaking into groups, each with a fishbowl, managers and supervisors and their teams share their stories and discuss the communication challenges they face. A notetaker is assigned. Onlookers are asked to look for and then summarize themes (which can then be matched to the notes for triangulation later if useful).

## Round 3

Employees engage in this story-based inquiry process by sharing their stories one by one, each taking 1 minute and timing themself. As a group, they discuss the communication challenges they face without their supervisors or managers present, and peers present the information back to the group (which can then be matched to the notes for triangulation later if useful).

## Leader Closing

Once all stories have been shared, this process could go in several directions, depending on goals and timing. Here are a few ideas:

1. Priority rankings are given to the top issues or recommended solutions on posters made from their story data.
2. Designated people share out the key themes they heard across the fishbowls for an open strategy session.
3. People map suggestions and solutions in creative and visual ways.
   - Generously thank people for their time and appreciate them for sharing their stories and listening with their hearts to each other's stories.
   - Explain the importance of confidentiality to psychological safety.
   - Let them know what next steps are in terms of follow-up, if any.

The presence of these stories is powerfully felt. This process creates an opportunity for leaders and colleagues to show up as active listeners who care about each other. This is a time to model the practices of institutional and interpersonal holding, so that people can feel seen, heard, and affirmed in sharing their stories.

## Tool 2: SEE: An Inner-Resource Cultivation Practice

Humanizing leaders understand what affects them emotionally and learn how to manage it. Understanding how cognitive and neural functioning mediate emotions during communication is essential to effectively navigate identity-related stress and support others to do the same. Cognitive neuroscience helps us understand people's physiological responses to emotional experiences, including the science behind the popularized, oft-misused term *trigger*. A trigger prompts strong feelings in sudden ways that can feel beyond our control in the moment; one feels besieged by emotion, unable to react in ways befitting our more practiced selves in calmer moments.

*Understanding how to navigate intense emotions is a vital leadership skill.* Importantly, our triggered reactions involve *projection*—we see unconscious aspects of ourselves in other people but believe the emotion we feel in the moment is entirely about them and their actions, not about us. Our reaction to projections is somatic—we feel it physically, even though it is outside our conscious awareness. For example, when an authority figure makes us feel a certain way, it surfaces old emotions about a parent's treatment of us, and yet we believe our feelings are caused by the present person only. Identifying projections takes practice, but, once you learn it, it is a superpower. Learning to identify these processes is life-changing for leaders, enabling them to pass on these vital professional skills. Buddha offers the grounding insight that, "All human unhappiness comes from not facing reality squarely, exactly as it is." Enter the need to face reality more productively.

*Triggers are useful the moment we decide they are.* Trigger moments correspond to early needs—attention, acceptance, appreciation, affection, and allowing—that remain unresolved and surface in the present (Richo, 2019). These moments are a departure from our more practiced ways of being. Trigger moments, when viewed as opportunities for self-learning, help us in our work to create increased self-awareness. This builds through reflecting on intense emotional responses with honesty. Reflection in our triggers is a leadership cultivation practice that increases our capacity for responsiveness. It is useful to know that there are trigger archetypes: (1.) feeling self-conscious, (2.) feeling discounted, (3.) feeling controlled, (4.) feeling taken advantage of, (5.) feeling vulnerable, (6.) boundary concerns, (7.) feeling uncomfortable, and (8.) fearing what might happen (Richo, 2019). Understanding these can help leaders identify and consider them in real time.

*Through the SEE* practice, *leaders learn to slow down reactive emotions* so that events that were once emotionally fraught no longer trigger overpowering reactions. Rather, they are met with a pause, an intentional response of space building (rather than an automatic reaction), and then a response. Creating an inner space between any stimulus and our response to it (à la Viktor Frankl in the previous chapter) and using the space to reflect on the original experience affirm feelings we felt as *younger us* so they can be resolved when new stressors present. When we do this, once troubling and confusing behaviors take leave of us. Reflecting helps us realize, for example, that intense anger eclipses more useful—though more uncomfortable—emotions such as sadness and grief, which we can then allow ourselves to feel to resolve intense emotional experiences and the thought–behavior patterns that ensue from them. This begets personal freedom.

When our inner resources to calmly withstand agitating stimuli are activated, the emotional part of our brain (the adrenal system) is quieted, which creates an access point into the reasoning part of our brain (the limbic system). Engaging this process helps us develop trust in ourselves and faith in our ability to access inner resources to respond calmly to upsetting stimuli. Over time, we become practiced at creating this inner space, and it becomes automatic, even during times of acute stress. This is adaptive leadership at its best—enabling leaders to build the here-and-now *and* the future with tenacity, humility, and curiosity in ways that elevate everyone.

As people grow up, our unique socialization conditions us to believe in storied versions of ourselves and how the world works. It is vital to engage in unlearning the damaging parts of these storied versions of us to pursue our growth as leaders. The concept of the *emotional imagination*—the meeting place of cognitive, creative, and reflexive dimensions of the psyche—is enormously useful. Imagination as a cognitive process invokes psychological imagery; it involves how people conceptualize, create, and envision reality and possibilities. Emotional imagination shapes how people feel, visualize, make meaning of, and understand themselves and the world, through the nexus of experiences that shape our thinking without notice or conscious processing.

We harness our *emotional imagination* to create inner space for conscious examination, finding parts of ourselves that have been folded in, concealed. Conscious examination helps us grow past behavior patterns that no longer serve us well. As children, we were not independent enough to be agentic in naming our experiences or in how we indexed narratives about ourselves based on those experiences. Events happened to us; we were interpreted and narrated by others with more power than us; they told us stories of who we are, and we saw this as Truth. As children, we have little control over what happens to us or how we interpret it. As adults, we have agency we can now use to engage our emotional imagination as a portal to re-storying ourselves, which opens possibilities to transcend current norms and opportunities. This is revelatory.

*Emotional imagination* is a vital growth concept. Emotions shape our thought patterns, and vice versa, as mutually reinforcing aspects of memory, cognitive functioning, and learning. This is particularly salient to building a sense of personal agency, which leaders do through unlearning and relearning (i.e., changing and building) their storied selves, limiting thought patterns, internal dialogues, beliefs, and cognitive distortions generated over time. The concept of emotional imagination helps leaders engage in learning about how our experiences were laid down as memory, how thought patterns shape self-understanding, how childhood influences shape our stories of ourselves (consciously and unconsciously). This helps us imagine beyond the confines of current indoctrination to create forward on our own terms. Freedom.

Cultivating awareness of physiological responses to triggers builds reflexive capacity and self-management skills. Humans do not tend to accurately read how their own experiences, emotions, and identities play out, how their behaviors, assumptions, and biases stem from unconscious beliefs about themselves and expectations of others and the world. For leaders, understanding implicit biases has performance implications. Learning to re-story oneself leads to more intentional choice-making and liberation from harmful social constructions that corrode healthy communication if not attended to. This is learning and leadership as a practice of freedom (hooks, 1994).

Leaders experience liberation from engaging their emotional imagination to process and revise formative life experiences and the beliefs, cognitive distortions, and patterns of thinking and behavior they shape. Tremendous benefit comes when leaders learn to notice and be curious about (rather than judgmental of) interpretations that no longer serve them well (as byproducts of old storied versions of them). One example of an obstructive emotion is shame, a ubiquitous yet often hidden emotion that drives people to act in ways that do not align with their aspirational selves. When they learn to work with their shame, rather than avoid or defend against it (often with anger or tears), they gain the power to re-story themselves, to rewrite constraining narratives that help them to cultivate a more receptive sensibility than otherwise possible. To uplift everyone in mission mode, rewriting otherwise constraining narratives must be embedded in organizational learning processes.

SEE enables the kinds of intentional reflection that help leaders identify how projection happens between people—including them and those around them. Projection is what causes people to react to things not actually happening in the moment. Clearing this familiar noise in everyone's head enables presence to read, interpret, and make decisions about situations at hand more accurately. It is powerful for leaders to come to a clearer understanding of the social constructions, thought patterns, and socialization processes that shape their leadership. The key is learning to understand what was messaged, implicitly and explicitly, to see how other people's perspectives and values shaped their sense of self, their expectations, their logics and decision-making processes, and their relational style.

Leaders with a humanizing mindset cultivate a working understanding of how emotional habits shape thinking, and specifically how limiting thoughts, when constructively challenged, can be processed to resolution. Limiting thoughts, as false beliefs, cause both inner and relational misattunement. The good news is that limiting thoughts can be reshaped. Leaders, teams, and organizations can learn to identify the emotional register of specific experiences and interactions through conscious re-storying; this is accomplished through reflection and dialogic engagement—a process for intentional thought partnership, dialogue, and self-reflection (Ravitch & Carl, 2019). Once people see the impact this has on communication and decision-making, this becomes internalized as a mindset.

A humanizing mindset enables people to challenge their past experiences, storied selves, and false beliefs (e.g., "dissent is disrespect" or "needing help is weakness") formed through messaging and life experience, often through the veil of transference and projection, and imprinted on the psyche as fact during their developmental years by people who had power over them and whom they needed to survive. Leaders learn to see their own cognitive distortions and thought patterns as well as those of the people around them—people's filters are reused over the course of their lives through unconscious projection and transference, which continue unless they are interrupted through their conscious reckoning with them.

Leaders must learn to *undoctrinate* themselves—attend to deflections, misunderstandings, cognitive distortions, and unexamined biases as openings to seeing themselves more clearly, understanding the work they still must do to move beyond their own limiting beliefs. The ability to identify and extract logics that harm is foundational to humanizing leadership.

Clinical psychologist and bestselling author David Richo's (2019) *Triggers: How We Can Stop Reacting and Start Healing* offers a portable process acronym—**SEE**: shadow, ego, early life—to understand the psychological processes that lead people to becoming triggered. SEE is an entry point into a customized stress management plan. Here's a distillation of Richo's SEE model:

- **Shadow:** Characteristics, desires, impulses, and attitudes we have repressed, disavowed, or denied because they were deemed problematic, or threatening are considered our *shadow side*. We do not acknowledge or admit to these traits or feelings, and so they remain hidden from our conscious awareness. When we observe these traits in others, we react with criticism or anger. Shadowing keeps this away from our conscious thought. Thus, these traits remain out of our reach for identification, working through, and resolution. Our reaction to a triggering event, in fact, points us to something we have not yet admitted to or seen in ourselves, something that needs to be integrated into our self-understanding. Our shadow side creates a lens of projection; thus, *we see others as we project them to be*.

- **Ego:** The ego is inflated when we see ourselves as better than or above others, believe we deserve more, or feel entitled to better than other people. When we feel disrespected or slighted, this can trigger feelings of indignation or anger in us. Underneath these emotions is fear of being found to be less than who we think we are, of losing our entitlement to honor, recognition, inclusion, or status. Our reaction of indignation shows us the growth work we can do. We build a healthy ego by letting go of our inflated entitlements, understanding that ego steers us away from our most compassionate and relational parts. Once we pop the bubble of self-importance, we open ourselves up to feel deeper humility, self-awareness, compassion, and connection with others. The ego is the lens of entitlement; we see each other in accord with what we expect or demand.
- **Early life:** Distressing and traumatic early life experiences condition our psychology. Triggers tap into deep unresolved feelings from experiences with parents or early caregivers, times when we were not attended to, accepted, or affirmed, when our emotional needs were not appreciated. Many of us, as children, storied ourselves negatively to avoid seeing that those who were supposed to affirm and protect us did not. These early experiences can create a well of pain that, if touched, splashes up into the present. We transfer feelings and expectations that apply to people in our past onto those in our present unknowingly, which is confusing because it feels like it is about them. Early life becomes the lens of transference—we unknowingly put old faces onto people in our current life instead of healing those old wounds so that we can be present.

*SEE unlocks our own growth and healing.* Leaders build a sense of self-trust when they learn to identify their own triggers and position them as a gateway to resolving unresolved emotions through identifying their hold on thinking, choices, and behavior. Humanizing leaders address these unconscious motivators rather than kicking the unresolved-issue can down the road. This is about calming our nervous systems, quieting our negative self-talk, and questioning our judgment of others, which needs to happen to examine and shift our habits of mind and heart.

The *SEE* process, over time, engenders the ability to re-see ourselves and the people around us, the people who matter to us, in ways that are more accurate because they are grounded in an authentically contextualized sense of reality. It is about the process of becoming curious about, rather than judgmental or critical of, our own familiar thought patterns, sedimented cognitive distortions, and invisible machinations of mind and habit that shape our decision-making processes and daily states of mind and mood. In this sense, it is about rewriting our life stories through a resource rather than deficit lens. It is about pushing into binaries that confine our thinking and finding a both/and (rather than an either/or) way of understanding people and situations that allows for complexity and adaptation.

Triggers announce our work to us—surfacing what is unresolved within us so that we can finally work it through to healthy resolution (Richo, 2019). Unresolved pain within us requires focused internal work, and dialogic engagement with others can help us unpack our own interpretations since we cannot see how influential our own beliefs are, like a fish in water. As a practice, writing reflectively and talking with others surfaces what is invisible to us.

As American T.V. icon Mr. Rogers offers,

> Anything that's human is mentionable, and anything that is mentionable can be more manageable. When we can talk about our feelings, they become less overwhelming, less upsetting, and less scary. The people we trust with that important talk can help us know that we are not alone.

'Mentionability' of inner experiences is the heart of a humanizing mindset. Self-growth involves identifying, naming, and sharing distress so that others can help us expand and reframe our thinking, growing through learning alternative viewpoints and through accompaniment, a form of institutional holding in times of distress and uncertainty.

*The past is done with you as soon as you are done with the past.* Read that again—it is a liberating phrase said by a client. Painful emotions live large in our subconscious; we let them stay rent-free, rarely questioning their presence. These negative emotions surface to our conscious mind during a triggered response to experiences that reverberate old, difficult feelings (i.e., feeling invisible or unheard as a child, feelings of shame induced by parents and others). People can feel distress and confusion when their reactions are disproportionate to an event (a good indication that it is a trigger moment). These moments are harbingers of liberatory possibility. Without this conscious intrusion of painful feelings, they would remain estranged, stuck in the hidden realm of assumptions, implicit biases, and tacit beliefs that, unknowingly yet powerfully, shape how we view, interpret, and experience the world, the workplace, and ourselves.

Staying present with strong negative feelings to use them as tools—barometer, compass, failsafe, cooling system, chisel—changes our fundamental relationship with emotions, taking their harmful power away. Change in this realm means that we learn to show up for ourselves by giving ourselves the five As—attention, acceptance, appreciation, affection, and allowing—rather than expecting others to do this for us (Richo, 2019). This empowers us since we are no longer unknowingly controlled by past hurts and unmet needs—we have released ourselves from them by acknowledging and feeling (rather than avoiding and dismissing) them. Leaders are liberated when they engage difficult emotions and distress as growth work and liberating when they teach those around them to do the same.

Humanizing leadership requires the ability to critically read self—which necessitates making trigger moments and the earlier experiences that form their foundation conscious to ourselves. This means examining our (and others') socially constructed beliefs, priorities, and expectations that have been messaged to us both directly and indirectly and, further, identifying the value hierarchies that were taught to us as universal. These socially constructed messages and value hierarchies may be made up, but they became our vision and version of self. Therefore, it takes focused self-reflection to uncover the hidden layers of our thoughts, feelings, and behavior patterns (Richo, 2019). This work is a game changer for leadership and organizations.

Workplaces are collection sites for people's emotions, for better and worse. Developing inner resources to foment internal freedom builds an ever-widening practice of calmness and compassion to self. Expanding compassion creates the ability to harness, rather than be controlled by, one's own emotions—to use them as material for focused self-development. Developing an understanding of their socialized beliefs, values, and triggers through intentional storytelling practices helps people learn to re-story themselves in generative ways. Humanizing leaders choose to be actively conscious and calm—As former Indian Prime Minister Indira Gandhi avers, "still in the midst of activity and to be vibrantly alive in repose".

## Tool 3: SEEing Projections

Building on the practice of **SEE**, leaders can productively engage the psychological concept of *projection*—we project onto people as we are projected upon—regularly and without conscious acknowledgement. Projection, a psychological term, means taking an internal map we have already established and using it as the lens through which we view and come to understand the world. As Hugh Prather (1972) avers, "No matter what we talk about, we are talking about ourselves."

When we engage in **projection**, we misinterpret what is inside of us as coming from outside, meaning another person. Generally, projection forms the basis of empathy through our projection of our personal experiences to understand another's subjective experience. In its negative form, it is a defense mechanism in which the ego defends itself against highly negative parts of the self (sometimes referred to as disowned) by denying their existence within themselves and attributing them to others, which breeds misunderstanding and mistrust and causes harm. For example, a workplace bully may project their own feelings of vulnerability onto a target, or someone who is confused may project their feelings of confusion and inadequacy onto another person unknowingly.

Projection uses blame shifting and attempts to induce shame in others. Projection is an early phase of introjection when others use their established maps and apply them to us without their conscious awareness. Without intentional reflection, how their map is communicated may even make us take their expectations on as our own—we take on their negative projections as if they are ours. This is as common as breathing; understanding how this process works is enormously clarifying and liberating for leaders and teams. These frames help leaders to engage with the concept of projection:

- **What we see depends on how we see:** The ability to conceptualize and understand how we "show up"—as in how we are seen by others—is hard won. People typically assume too much about the people around us *because we project*, discussed in Chapter One. Understanding the human condition of projection drives our self-knowledge and promotes our healthy functioning.
- **We do not see ourselves accurately:** We do not see ourselves accurately in terms of how our social identities play out socially, relationally, and professionally, how our thoughts and behaviors stem from our unconscious understandings of self, other, and the world which are conditioned and subjective. This leaves our unexamined parts flapping in the proverbial wind. Through this projection practice, leaders and teams become more conscious, thoughtful, and intentional of how we present ourselves and show up in the professional realm.
- **We do not see others accurately:** Just as we do not see ourselves accurately because of the human condition of projection, we often see others inaccurately given how we project our expectations onto them. This can be subtle, such as seeing a behavior as unprofessional when it is our personal preference or issue. People come to understand others better when they can see them through the prism of empathy. The ability to read and respond in resonant ways, in the moment, is called emotional intelligence, which is a superpower.
- **Challenging projections is bedrock professional development:** Practice challenging your projections and cognitive distortions—thoughts that cause individuals to perceive reality inaccurately—in an everyday way to learn to identify and undo them as a form of professional self-reflection and development. This work must sometimes be solo and other times must be relational and even team-based work.
- **Unlearning requires change and loss:** Unlearning takes focused effort and it generates discomfort and a sense of loss (of the ego variety). Relearning feels energizing and restorative; it is not additive: it is necessarily transformative—people reconstruct stories of self to identify embedded mythologies and to supplant them with new truths and resonant possibilities. It is the hallmark of a growth mindset to realize the incredible power of unlearning and relearning.
- **It's all about framing:** In the ability to reframe negative experiences to pull out the growth and lessons lies personal freedom. In resisting the default mode of bombarding self with negative messages upon a misstep or struggle lies the possibility of giving ourselves new ways of seeing even that which we are used to seeing as negative or misunderstanding. How people frame things is how we see them. This includes how we frame ourselves.
- **Feed the good wolf:** The negative self-talk we subject ourselves to is part of the human condition. Negative self-talk is how we turn deficit orientations onto ourselves, which in turn creates an unconscious foundation for the way we look at the world. When we feel that we ourselves are deficient

because we have needs, because we think it is bad to be imperfect, or for whatever reasons we come up with (that are subjective and imprinted on us), then the extension of this condition is that we look at others that way and feel we need to shore ourselves up because we feel lesser. These deficit orientations are imprinted on us, an introject we carry with us without our conscious awareness. This Cherokee story speaks powerfully to how our framing shapes how we see reality and ourselves:

A Cherokee grandfather was speaking with his grandson,

"Son," he said, "Within all of us there is a battle of two wolves. One is evil. He is anger, envy, jealousy, sorrow, regret, greed, arrogance, self-pity, guilt, resentment, inferiority, lies, false pride, superiority, and ego."

He continued, "The other wolf is good. He is joy, peace, love, hope, serenity, humility, kindness, benevolence, empathy, generosity, truth, compassion, and faith."

"The same fight is going on inside of you, and inside every other person, too," explained the elder.

The grandson thought about it and then asked his grandfather, "Which wolf will win?"

The grandfather replied, "The one you feed."

- Without consciously knowing it, most of us feed our bad inner wolf—our time, energy, and focus. We give our negative thinking too much power. Working to see our projections frees us from the habituated behavior of feeding the bad wolf that exists within everyone, ever hungry and clamoring within our minds to be fed. Seeing this is about understanding that we have power to choose where to put our focus and energy. It also suggests that we must be quite intentional about increasing our positive self-talk to help create balance.
- **Framing is everything:** Peter Kuriloff, a close colleague and organizational psychologist who has worked with corporate leaders for 5 decades, shares this story about the power of framing: An elderly woman living in an old age home is labeled "needy, delusional, and attention seeking" by resentful staff who report that she "acts crazy and thinks she is God." A new doctor arrives and speaks with the woman, asking questions instead of assuming the staff's framing of the situation was the whole picture. Through humanizing inquiry, the doctor learned that the woman did not think she was God, but, rather, that her son had told her they could always connect through God just

before he died. This insight radically reframed the woman's behavior from 'attention seeking' to 'connection seeking.' This reframe enabled the staff to see her through an assets rather than a deficit lens. Her so-called behavior issues vanished. Framing is everything: When the purview widened, through humble inquiry, the negative dynamics changed. Framing shapes reality: Our thoughts become us. Change your thinking and you change the world around you and within you. Widen your aperture to deepen understanding.

- **Embrace misunderstanding:** Humans live in a state of perpetual misinterpretation, projection, and misunderstanding. Only by understanding this do we open the space to see how interpretations are shaped by our social identities, histories, experiences, and power differentials. How people understand themselves, others, and the world around them is an implicit yet powerful part of all interpretive action, upon which everything we do is based. Likewise, people understand present and future events based on what and how they have known to the present, including how they have known themselves. In turn, their interpretations of present and future events revise, to some extent, the way they see themselves, others, and the world. From this perspective, the systematic deconstruction of their interpretations is an ethical responsibility because it allows for increased understanding of the values and biases that underlie and direct their efforts (Nakkula & Ravitch, 1998).

## Tool 4: Implicit Bias Checks

**Implicit biases** are the attitudes and stereotypes that affect our understanding, interpretations, behavior, and decisions *unconsciously*. These biases are activated involuntarily, without our awareness or intentional control. Residing deep in the subconscious, implicit biases are different from known biases we may choose to conceal for the purposes of fulfilling obligations of social or political correctness. In contrast, *our implicit biases are not accessible to us through introspection*. The implicit bias associations in our subconscious shape our feelings and attitudes about other people based on how we interpret their social identities or appearance.

Bias associations develop through exposure to direct and indirect messages by influential people in our lives and the media which, over, time, condition our thinking and frames for interpreting the world. Implicit biases are:

- **Unconscious:** We cannot access our biases directly, no matter the effort.
- **Pervasive:** Everyone has implicit biases, despite avowing impartiality.
- **Misaligned:** Implicit biases do not align with our espoused beliefs or values.
- **Drivers:** Implicit biases drive our behavior unconsciously.
- **Weighted:** Implicit biases tend to favor our own ingroup/s unconsciously.
- **Malleable:** Implicit biases can be unlearned through self-reflection and practice.

Adaptive equity-oriented institutions proactively identify risk areas where implicit biases tend to affect behavior, decisions, and judgment. Instituting bias reporting structures, clear procedures for hiring and decision-making, accountability structures, and meaningful professional development that foments awareness of implicit bias helps mitigate the frequency and degree to which people act from biases contrary to their conscious values and beliefs. It is as Jennifer Eberhardt (2019) says: "Moving forward requires continued vigilance. It requires us to constantly attend to who we are, how we got that way, and all the selves we have the capacity to be."

The questions below can help foster reflection and professional development.

## Implicit Bias Self-Reflection Questions

1. What explicit biases do I hold? How were they formed? Are they useful now?
2. What implicit biases have been pointed out to me over time? By whom? At what periods in my life? Are there common threads? Do I agree on some level?
3. How might my implicit biases play out in my leadership? Any examples?
4. How do I *feel* about workplace equity?
5. Who can help me identify and address my implicit biases productively?
6. Do I hold deficit orientations about specific social identity/professional groups?
7. If so, where do these come from? Are they factually correct (as in backed up by data)? Do they block my impartiality?
8. What excites, frustrates, challenges, motivates me in professional discussions about equity, diversity, or identity? Why is this the case?
9. Am I aware of how my social identity (i.e., intersections of my race, gender, culture, religion) shapes my thinking? Shapes how I show up?
10. How do my priorities shape the company's professional development offerings?

## Crucial Concepts for Seeing Implicit Biases

As chief learner, it is crucial to remember that workplace conversations relating to identity, bias, and equity, which center around people's race, social class/caste, gender, religion, and other aspects of identity, can be activating to some people. Adaptive leaders need to create a bespoke glossary of working concepts that help them, their team, and their organizations effectively plan for and navigate conversations on topics that can be upsetting, triggering, or tense. The concepts included here are useful in conversations about implicit bias and workplace equity. These concepts are introduced here and revisited in Chapter 5, Equity Mindset.

- **Microaggressions** are common, brief, verbal, behavioral, or environmental indignities, intentional or unintentional, that communicate negative, hostile, invalidating, or derogatory slights and insults toward people of color and other non-dominant identity groups. Those who commit microaggressions are rarely aware of their impact because what they have said stems from their implicit (and thus not consciously accessible to them) biases. This concept, created by social psychologist Derald Wing Sue, teaches people to identify, understand, and communicate ways that daily interactions affect people from non-dominant groups.
- **Intersectional identities** are based on the seminal critical legal theory created by Kimberlé Crenshaw about how different forms of identity-based discrimination intersect in relation to structural discrimination. The concept is that an individual's identity consists of multiple intersecting factors, including, but not limited to, gender identity, gender expression, race, ethnicity, social class, religious beliefs, and sexual identity and expression. All people have at least two intersections (race and gender), and some have more along the bias lines of privilege and disadvantage (i.e., being Black and a woman, a White man who is gay, being mixed race, ethnicity, culture, religion, and so on); people should be recognized in the complex ways they identify rather than in identity boxes.
- **Identity-based stress/racial stress** is stress produced by identity-based racialized experiences that cause psychological, emotional, and/or physical stress. One can extend this concept to gender, social class/caste, indeed all intersectional identities. The concept of identity-based stress helps people understand the specific physiological responses people have to conversations about and/or interactions about race, social class, ethnicity, and so on. Everyone has a racial identity, and thus racial stress, and a broader identity, thus identity-based stress more broadly, whether taught that we do or not. The scope of this runs along axes of identity and structural discrimination.
- **Racial literacy** is the ability to read, recast, and resolve racially stressful encounters. *Reading* means decoding racial subtexts, sub-codes, and scripts. *Recasting* means reducing stress in racially stressful encounters using racial mindfulness. *Resolving* means negotiating racially stressful encounters toward a healthy conclusion. Racial literacy enables people to build tools they can immediately employ during identity-based stress encounters (Stevenson, 2014). Racial literacy development, when done well, is intersectional in approach.

There is no panacea for handling stress that emerges during conversations about identity and inequity at work; however, building tools helps you facilitate discussions in ways that create an open and communicative milieu, a safe emotional environment that can help prevent or de-escalate tensions. Improving your own racial literacy is necessary to support others to do the same. It helps to build and sustain an ethos that is unafraid to examine issues of inequity and that can do so productively. This is picked back up in Chapter 5, Equity Mindset.

## Tool 5: Build Relational Trust and Create Psychological Safety

**Relational trust** is built through day-to-day social exchanges and evinces a shared sense of imperative to take on the challenging work of complex adaptive change. Relational trust fosters the organizational conditions for individuals to initiate and sustain the kinds of activities necessary to effect productivity improvements (Bryk & Schneider, 2002). Building relational trust includes facilitating accountability for shared standards while allowing people autonomy and mutual support. This reduces the vulnerability employees feel when asked to take on tasks connected to honest communication, authenticity in the workplace, or diversity, equity, and inclusion (DEI) efforts. This facilitates the psychological safety necessary for adaptive change.

To build relational trust, create dialogic engagement groups within or across teams. Follow these steps or customize the process:

1. Introduce the concept of relational trust.
2. Offer the framework of BRAVING introduced earlier in this chapter.
3. Discuss why trust matters in the organization today.
4. Build knowledge about what constitutes relational trust and lack thereof.
5. Create a shared definition of trust and description of why it is important. This helps examine ways that people carry their own unexamined definitions of trust.
6. Gather and analyze quick data on trust through rapid-cycle inquiry.
7. Share the rapid-cycle inquiry findings and solicit possible next steps.
8. Act.

To create psychological safety, create dialogic engagement groups within or across teams. Follow these steps or customize the process:

1. Lead by example. Leaders must set an example of what psychological safety looks like for the rest of the organization. If done properly, behaviors such as institutional and interpersonal holding become normative.
2. Ask for consistent upward flow of feedback.
3. Acknowledge your mistakes with transparency and demand others do the same.
4. Solicit a range of opinions, including those that differ from yours.
5. Be approachable and encourage people to ask questions and share feedback.
6. Model and encourage active listening.

At the group behavior level, people feel valued and that they can contribute to the team when they feel listened to, seen, and affirmed. Ideas include:

- Leave phones at the door or turned off during meetings.
- Show understanding by checking for meaning.
- Encourage sharing by asking questions and sharing confusion.
- Actively ask for the opinions of those who are quiet.
- Co-create a safe environment for risk-taking and sharing of ideas.

To achieve psychological safety, people must feel comfortable voicing their opinions, challenges, and needs without fear of being judged. To develop a safe environment, create ground rules for interaction. For example:

- Do not interrupt each other.
- Accept all ideas equally without judgment.
- Do not blame or shame.
- Encourage suggestions and listen to them with care.
- Respond to input from others constructively.
- View feedback to strengthen ideas and processes.
- Normalize a multiplicity of voices around decision-making.

Psychological safety is vital to ensuring a healthy organizational ethos in which everyone feels able to contribute their ideas and be authentic. As Winnicott (1960) states, "The alternative to being is reacting, and reacting interrupts being and annihilates."

## Humanizing Mindset Practices

### *Try Today*

1. **Free-write:** Begin with a free-write, which is a quick, stream-of-consciousness way to get thoughts onto paper. Consider what makes you feel humanized and then what you wish for people you care about for their workplace experiences. Reflect on which dimensions of humanization you can bring to life.
2. **Leader journal:** Choose a journal to write in or, if you prefer the digital mode, open a new file on your phone or laptop for leader journaling. This can be in the form of free-writes to prompts, pulse reflections on events or conversations, or reflections while triggered to learn from what you are thinking and feeling as an event or interaction is happening or just happened.
3. **Disseminate pulse surveys:** and then engage in data review and accountability checks with team members.

4. **Find an accountabilibuddy** for backstage processing related specifically to creating a humanizing workplace. This is discussed in Chapter Five.
5. **Trust-building session:** Use your next regularly scheduled meeting as a trust-building session. Ask: How can we humanize ourselves, each other, and the workplace? Consider small groups and report-outs so people can share comfortably and the knowledge gets to the group for consideration.

## Build a Weekly Practice

1. The practice of self-reflection relies on dialogic engagement, so find an accountabilibuddy for peer mentoring and work together to train your minds to learn how to view typical workplace arrangements as potentially problematic in ways that are both appreciative and solutionary.
2. Build an inquiry group model to support ongoing learning about humanizing processes, policies, and practices.

## Try Monthly

1. Practice using humanizing language in emails even for seemingly inconsequential correspondences. Hold yourself accountable to acknowledge people's humanity when you communicate and engage.
2. Make affirmation an agenda item at the start of every meeting.
3. Organize a monthly brown-bag series for people to share their ideas and expertise on things they know best—this opens opportunities for knowledge sharing and collaboration.
4. Revisit policies to determine what can be made more friendly and intuitive. Eliminate policies, norms, and language that undermine people's humanity.
5. At the end of every month, write down and acknowledge what worked and what went right; reevaluate what did not. Share in meetings and communications.

# 3

# SYSTEMS MINDSET

## What Is a Systems Mindset?

A systems mindset prioritizes the relatedness between components working together to perform defined functions to advance an objective over the individual components themselves, with the individual as a single broad-minded lever operating within a network of interdependent parts. The more transparent the system, the deeper the service to larger organizational and workplace goals, priming the individual to default to observing problems in their wider context and to examine underlying structures. Leyla Acaroglu (2017) describes this as an interplay of five elements—interconnectedness, synthesis, emergence, feedback loops, and causality:

- **Interconnectedness,** the first element, relies on ongoing analysis of connected parts to inform decision-making. Moving from linear 'if–then' logic to messier 'both–and' logic requires disciplined, sustained consideration and critical interrogation of dynamic, chaotic, interwoven relationships.
- **Synthesis,** the second element, is the continual combination of two or more seemingly disparate parts to create something new. Unlike reductionist tendencies to break down, dissect, or deconstruct a problem, synthesis demands a holistic approach to understanding phenomena and treats understanding of the whole *and* the parts equally. Foregrounding the relationships and connections between parts rather than focusing on each distinct part is the act of synthesis, which involves the ability to recognize and activate interconnectedness.
- **Emergence,** the third element, focuses on the self-organization of individual parts of a system, reflecting the embodiment of the interactions of

DOI: 10.4324/b23253-4

those parts. From a systems perspective, as larger things constantly emerge from smaller parts, the natural outcome of purposely bringing components together reflects synergies of those parts. This reinforces non-linearity and self-organization.

- **Feedback loops,** the fourth element, act as points of entry through which individuals activate, observe, understand, and intervene in systems. The two primary types of feedback loops, *reinforcing* loops and *balancing* loops, combine in an infinite variety of ways to produce the complex systems within which we work. The first (*reinforcing*) produces both growth and decay. That is, it compounds change in one direction with even more change. For example, in an employee–supervisor reinforcing loop, positive reinforcement from the supervisor can produce good employee performance, while negative reinforcement can lead to poor employee performance.

- A *balancing* **feedback** loop allows for the balancing of system parts and continuous recalibration. Balancing loops resist further increases in each direction in that they bring things to a desired state and keep them there, much like a thermostat regulates the temperature. An adaptive leader who appreciates and understands feedback loops deepens perspective on correlational and causal relationships within a dynamic space and can effectuate decisions with this perspective in mind.

- **Causality,** the fifth element, reflects a leader's understanding of feedback loops and their ability to lend clarity around how one thing results in another thing—deciphering influences—within a dynamic and constantly evolving system. Understanding causality through purposeful practice enables leaders to validate organizational responses and deepens perspective on agency, leading to the rewarding and lifting of some connections and relationships and the downplaying and possible dismantling of others.

Leaders who practice a systems mindset interrogate unquestioned relational logics by moving beyond component parts and toward a more transparent whole. Inquiry and humanizing mindsets help leaders activate key conditions for a systems mindset to connect broad-based strategic and day-to-day operational goals with an ethos of care through compassion and appreciative listening.

## Cultivating a Systems Mindset

In organizations of all sizes, multiple systems work in tandem, ideally harmoniously, to consistently achieve intended objectives. Examining and appreciating interconnectivity signal the priority given to horizontal cross-organizational discoveries and rediscoveries that cut across verticals (departments, roles, functions). Cultivating a systems mindset signals purposeful identification, sharing, and leveraging of vital cross-organizational understandings, perspectives, experiences, and needs to inform adaptive change.

A systems mindset enables leaders to support individuals and teams by holding both purpose and possibility: holding purpose through reflection and visible activation and messaging of organizational missions, and holding possibility by remaining open to and explicit about new ways of achieving it. It is this intersection that makes possible problem-solving processes that fit today's adaptive challenges and welcomes leaders to approach challenges more expansively. One way that leaders do this is via organization-wide shared practices of observing, interpreting, and intervening through targeted sense-making, with 'root-to-tip' confrontation of problems from multiple vantage points:

1. What are the *motivations for* this decision?
2. What are the *implications of* this decision?
3. Which of the relationships between component parts—which organizational structures (practices, policies, processes)—make possible and/or inhibit this decision?
4. What relationships will change/be impacted by this decision?
5. Which component parts can or should be adapted in relation to the system as a whole? Which parts can or should be wholesale adopted?
6. What is our rationale for each adaptation/adoption?

Nurturing shared decision-making, responsibility, and accountability comes through creating horizontal, internal functions the core purpose of which is to design and optimize systems-wide shared practices, values, and processes. These processes, as exemplified later in this chapter with tools such as logic modeling, recognize organizational complexities and promote new approaches to change. Scaffolding purpose and possibility through distributed leadership lifts common changing realities. Without a systems mindset, the logic between systems components is either nonexistent or unclear and can render solvable problems unactionable.

## Why Do Leaders and Organizations Need a Systems Mindset?

Organizational challenges can carry with them assumptions that some external force or event was either a cause or contributor. A systems mindset offers an alternative—namely, that internal structures and relationships *between* those structures are a first stop, and their importance is greater than or equal to the potential for an external force or event to generate or contribute to the problem. As Sonya Renee Taylor (2021) shares, "Systems do not maintain themselves; even our lack of intervention is an act of maintenance. Every structure in every society is upheld by the active and passive assistance of other human beings." Examining internal systems to uncover leverageable relationships demands routine reflection:

1. Who is in this system?
2. How is that changing over time?
3. How do people interpret their own roles and responsibilities, and how are people held accountable for them?
4. What impact do I as a leader have on how people interpret their work within systems?
5. What forces are at play that conflate, conflict, or compete with those perceptions and realities?

This backdrop—the iterative examination of systems structures linked to specific associated events to inform patterns of behavior—requires sustained inquiry into variables of interest (this is a purposeful practice). The way the organization staffs projects, markets products, identifies and raises revenue, commands market share, and focuses on changing needs, interests, and objectives over time enables leaders to uncover intentional intersectional perspectives, reveal relationships between parts, and predict patterns of behavior.

## Using a Systems Mindset to Approach Challenges

A leader with a systems mindset approaches challenge through underlying system structures to uncover causal loops and contributory behaviors, establishing a formative process of discovery. Examination and modification of underlying patterns of systems behavior require discipline to 'see the whole,' as outlined and demonstrated through Peter Senge's fifth discipline model, developed through fieldwork that he conducted as founder of the Center for Organizational Learning at MIT's Sloan School of Management.

Learning organizations require five key disciplines: *personal mastery, mental models, shared vision, team learning*, and *systems thinking* (Senge, 2012). A framework for seeing interrelationships and patterns of change rather than static snapshots and parts, systems thinking comprises a set of general principles, distilled time and the spanning of fields as diverse as the physical and social sciences, engineering and management. Complementing the disciplines are discipline-specific tools and techniques with origins in feedback, cybernetics, and engineering theory.

Systems thinking is core to building a learning organization, both standing on its own and embedded throughout each of the other four disciplines, divided according to primary focus on individuals and groups. Personal mastery, mental models, and systems thinking focus on individual behaviors and practices within an organization.

Personal mastery involves continually clarifying and deepening personal vision, focusing our energies, developing patience, and seeing reality objectively. Mental models are deeply ingrained assumptions that influence how we understand the world and how we act. Systems thinking focuses on interconnectedness. These three learning disciplines—personal vision, mental models, and systems thinking—all place the individual at the center of more complex relationships while emphasizing reflection and deliberation. Shared vision and team learning, by contrast, are inherently collective in nature, defined through activities engaged in by groups. Shared vision integrates individual goals into a collective organizational vision. The five disciplines are:

- **Personal mastery:** The discipline of holding a coherent image of personal vision within an assessment of current realities, personal mastery is a frame for how an individual views the world. Mastery originates from the Sanskrit root *mah*, or 'greater,' with Latin and Old English derivations eliciting domination over something ('I am your master'). The medieval French variation, *maître*, lends a different tone, one of exceptional skill or proficiency ('a master of craft'), with the idea of personal mastery aligning with this latter variation in its tribute not just to the production of results, but to the principles and personal development underlying their production.
- **Shared vision:** The discipline of leveraging consensus around and fostering commitment to mutual purpose. The discipline of shared vision involves the bringing together of disparate goals, values, and statements into alignment in support of experimentation and innovation. Without shared vision, leaders may revert to expediency and habit, twin risks inherent in fixed-information environments. Vision is not truly shared without adaptive change that propels leaders through recursive cycles of action and reflection, imbuing everyone with a stake in the others' success.
- **Mental models:** The discipline of valuing and activating reflection and honest inquiry to become more aware of the sources of our own thinking. Mental models clarify our own deeply held attitudes and perceptions of those around us, leading us to question and combat deeply ingrained assumptions.
- **Team learning:** The discipline of mobilizing energies and actions through dialogue and skillful discussion to achieve common goals and evince intelligence and ability greater than the sum of individual member contributions. Team learning is designed over time to get individuals thinking and acting *together* as opposed to thinking *alike*. At the heart of this discipline is the routine willingness to think and act as a living system, not by making point-in-time decisions or setting static roles and following through with discrete tasks, but instead via continuous conversation, with respect and deliberation, about what must be considered, addressed, and resolved. This discipline is based on the concept of alignment and, as such, carries the connotation of arranging scattered elements to function as a whole by orienting them to a common

awareness of each other, their purpose, and their current reality. This alignment develops when all feel committed to a common endeavor, starting with the ability to see and respect one another and to investigate mental models.

- **Systems thinking:** The discipline of studying system structures and behaviors, enriched by tools (some simple, others complex; some human-centered, others computer-modeled) that, over time, respond to non-linear aspects of daily life. When confronted with situations in which cause and effect do not occur in ways we anticipate, leaders practicing systems thinking build their own awareness of complexity, interdependencies, and change in service of maximal results with minimal expenditure.

As a form of adaptive leadership, systems thinking embraces individual and organizational adaptation to change to address challenges in novel ways. Mobilizing people who hold different definitions of a problem—and with them, different opinions about its root and its solution—to engage in a process of collaborative learning via different disciplines, perspectives, and parts of the organization can lead to entirely different ways of communicating.

A systems mindset moves leaders from 'How do we solve this?' to 'What's the nature of the issue we are trying to understand?' From 'How will the solution play out?' to 'What got us here? What will happen if left unaddressed?' Mapping key structural drivers of a dynamic promotes shifts in understanding so that what once seemed to be a 'big issue' suddenly is replaced by a new issue, previously uncovered and unexamined. Simulating 'How did we overlook that?' increases the likelihood of modeling similar decisions that might play out in the future.

### Practicing a Systems Mindset: Creating a Culture of Interconnectedness

One of the most powerful ways to establish interconnectedness is through a common vision. Honoring a richness of diverse perspectives and bridging into inclusive practices, a culture of interconnectedness recognizes that purpose brings people together in pursuit of a greater 'why?' Practicing a systems mindset in service of a culture of interconnectedness requires continuous discovery, purposeful uncovering of individual perceptions of a learning organization in accordance with the five learning disciplines. Integral to organizational health is a landscape within which people feel they can achieve their goals, where new models of thinking are being cultivated, and where collective purpose and ambition visibly drive both to support interconnected learning.

Operating within a model where all five principles work harmoniously to advance organizational learning requires coordination and dedication, imbuing a culture of interconnectedness through the promotion of an in-depth understanding of root causes and relationships between variables. Taking a collective approach to analyzing and synthesizing complex situations and phenomena through common codes of communication is core to these five practices:

1. *Articulate and socialize the alignment of individual and collective aspirations with a sharp focus on true organizational priorities,* initiating and instituting organizational change based on individual and collective *desire to change* rather than on any *need for change.*
2. *Routinely recognize and highlight complexities to see larger forces at play* in order to design and model transparent, testable expressions of complex organizational interrelationships.
3. *Sanction the testing of hypothesized relationships* with openness to resulting insights' potential to drive systems design and redesign so that the implication of change is understood, appreciated, and resourced.
4. *Drive purposeful, reflexive thinking and generative conversation* that raise awareness of deeply held assumptions and patterns of individual and collective behaviors.
5. *Predict the implications of individual and collective actions through interconnectedness, emergence, causality, and synthesis,* rendering purposeful connectivity between and among actors and actions and demonstrating relatability over time of the complexity of a problem or challenge. This deeper grasp of how the most vexing and seemingly intransigent organizational problems come about and shape-shift continuously informs perspective among changing circumstances and enables leaders to dedicate time and attention to those things that could be done differently to build coherence and commitment.

## Systems Mindset for Adaptive Change

A systems mindset requires cyclical stepping back in order to purposefully detect patterns and relationships to alternatively leverage or disrupt and to realize positive systemic change that embraces and honors ambiguity, uncertainty, and experimentation. Leading systems change requires audacity—to disrupt for the sake of alignment with purpose—and may entail the setting aside or reprioritizing of original objectives and shifting strategies as new opportunities emerge.

A systems mindset actively welcomes and solicits differing points of view from which one can design resonant narratives and facilitate conversations to explore distinct and even dissonant perspectives, undergirding core leadership competencies and skills. Following each leader skill/competency, in parentheses, is the learning discipline through which it can be realized.

- **Build trust:** Reserve time to understand and publicly mark progress toward shared goals to show active interest in people's concerns, issues, and challenges (learning discipline: shared vision).

- **Enable effective communication:** Promote and honor diverse points of view through deliberate and routine communications practices, identifying and celebrating common interests and celebrating perspectives distinct from their own (learning disciplines: mental models, team learning).
- **Focus on results:** Organize collaborative, transparent activities around shared results to illustrate and ensure that moving parts coalesce toward common aspirations rather than exist as unilateral or disjointed programmatic or sector goals (learning discipline: systems thinking).
- **Co-create support structures:** Enable individuals to work together in new ways for deeper idea exchange, data sharing and activation, and democratic decision-making. This cross-sectional/cross-functional/cross-role work codifies commitment to nimble, responsive governance structures (learning discipline: mental models).
- **Empower the collective:** Recognize and lift up individuals across all organizational levels who lead changes in their respective contexts that accentuate relationships to the whole (learning discipline: team learning).
- **Make clear/incentivize participation in systems:** Help individuals understand and articulate the benefits of participation through continuous refreshing of the value proposition for involvement and optimization (learning discipline: personal mastery).

## Example: Strategic Plan Relationship Alignment

A mid-sized nonprofit organization (budget $22 million USD) initiates its triannual 18-month strategic planning process. An outside consultancy (involved in both brand repositioning and in research and development of an innovative learning platform, for throughlines) is engaged to facilitate a three-phase work plan to articulate organizational aspirations through a joint statement of purpose and core value propositions. The phased plan is refined to reflect current-phase learnings and achievements, alongside a bold new shared vision. This process reinforces the systems mindset by empowering cross-departmental teams to ideate, prioritize, and weigh in on specific tactics that will enable delivery on these commitments to key stakeholders.

To activate the above, space is held for departmental and cross-departmental conversations during which opportunities are assessed and reviewed in detail, with ideation exercises designed to begin drafting and refining tactics that will be built up into an implementation plan, (re)opening horizontal pathways for knowledge transfer, production, and understanding, and prioritizing systemic relationships over individual components.

## Example: Logic Modeling for Continuous Improvement

A United States-based organization with seasonal staff turnover, highly localized data management, arm's-length relationships with major funders, and an under-developed programmatic theory of change, which resulted in resource misalignment vis-à-vis short- and long-term objectives.

As this disconnect between resource allocation and desired outcomes became clearer, senior leadership created a new internal position dedicated to evaluation and impact efforts. This signaled an embrace of a systems mindset by triangulating program planning, program delivery, and program evaluation; this was, specifically, to model shared logic supporting the relationships between long-term impact, shorter-term stakeholder outcomes, outputs, activities, and resources: See Figure 3.1.

To support the logic model, a measurement plan was created to map the proposed methodological approach—to align metrics or variables of interest; data collection tools for qualitative and quantitative data collection; intended change by stakeholder type considering context and assumptions; data sources; and an applied timeline—to program planning, implementation, and evaluation questions. See Figure 3.2.

This process revealed cross-departmental issues that had been misidentified as external—for example, shifting markets, lower participation—rather than internal. Mischaracterizing intended benefits led back to faulty program design. The process offered the rationale for, and assumptions behind, how relationships between components were prioritized, through which closed-loop thinking prevailed. The insights enabled the company to get beyond decontextualized and compartmentalized data to adapt.

To champion systemic information flow for continuous improvement, leadership designed a new role to reserve shared space to lead structured, facilitated staff engagement around developing and advanced relational understanding of

| RESOURCES | ACTIVITIES | OUTPUTS | SHORT-TERM OUTCOMES | LONG-TERM OUTCOMES |
|---|---|---|---|---|
| INPUTS we need to do proposed work | THINGS we do with resources identified | UNITS or VOLUME of production, based on Activities | CHANGES or BENEFITS to stakeholders in the near-term (<1 year) | IMPACT STATEMENTS / high-level change resulting from our work at scale |

FIGURE 3.1

| METRICS – Used to understand our progress | TARGETS – USED to determine if we're successful | TOOLS – To collect the data to be able to understand our progress | DATA SOURCES | DATA COLLECTION TIMELINE |
|---|---|---|---|---|

FIGURE 3.2

relationships between component parts. This signals a process of discovery and rediscovery that lies at the heart of a systems mindset.

## Learning Frames and Activations for a Systems Mindset

A first step in building a systems mindset recognizes professional practices, processes, and policies that support individual *and* collective aspirations and also cultivates current realities. Grounded in purposeful work of balancing and rebalancing vision, natural contextual shifts and evolutions make this first tool an important one.

### Tool 1: Personal Mastery Scan

A personal mastery scan raises one's awareness of the gap between current state and desired state. With this creative tension comes the incentive for continuous improvement and professional development. Individuals present their own vision, use their creative imagination, focus on learning with patience and perseverance, build self-knowledge, and guide themselves through self-control by routinely revisiting these questions:

1. In your *current* work environment, what daily interactions do you make sure transpire?
2. In your *ideal* work environment, what are the primary ways that you interact daily with others?
3. Which structures/systems tend to promote or hinder the interactions you describe above?
4. What proportion of your daily learnings are shaped by personal aspirations, what proportion by reality assessment, and what proportion by a convergence of both?

At the heart of a personal mastery scan is the deliberate cultivation of personal vision that is set among current realities. The gap between 'where I want to be' and 'where I am' creates a tension that, by its nature, seeks frequent revisiting for resolution. Creative and curious (versus reactive), aimed at personal growth, this scan can be characterized as passion imbued with inquisitive thinking, truth seeking, and resilience in service of a heightened ability to produce results through generative learning.

Using the personal mastery scan to inform shared vision ensures that you are bringing seemingly disparate goals, aspirations, and impact statements into alignment. A vision that is truly shared is rooted in an adaptable spirit that propels others through continuous improvement, a cycle of action, learning, and reflection. Sustaining this cycle requires leaders who communicate and interact through diverse channels, informal and formal, openly and freely. Shared vision sets the tone for individuals to feel they have a stake in others' success. Without shared vision, organizations risk reverting to expediency, efficiency, and habit. Support for shared vision draws on the concept of creative tension: a clear picture of current realities, a consistent and clear statement of desired outcomes, and, in consideration of both, collective decisions about how to proceed.

### Tool 2: Ladder of Inference

The third learning discipline for a systems mindset, *mental models*, lays bare the emotional, social, and ideological sources of our thinking. While building a habit of asking 'what happened here?' may, prima facie, feel unnatural, its inherent value lies in eliciting as many responses as there are respondents. As individuals, we variously interpret situations, our behavior and attitudes shaped by images, assumptions, and stories that we carry in our minds concerning ourselves, other people, and organizational structures and dynamics.

Because mental models are by their nature tacit, they are often untested and under-examined. Consider, as you read this, that you may not have noticed assumptions you implicitly read into each word, phrase, paragraph, page, chapter. The sheer profusion of mental models over time explains why people can observe the same event and describe it so differently or undergo the same experience and recount it so differently—they are paying attention to, and thereby valuing, distinctly different details while ignoring or devaluing others. The consequences of untested and unsurfaced mental models are unintended and potentially harmful outcomes.

Building and socializing a practice of recognizing—and publicly affirming, questioning, or dismantling—mental models bring into focus the metaphorical pane we use to reconstruct ways of seeing that conveniently serve evolving realities. Namely, our self-generating and reinforcing beliefs become based on faulty conclusions, inferred from what we 'see' and prioritizing those observations that retread past experience.

Our ability to achieve the results we desire is eroded by feelings that our beliefs are the truth, that the truth is obvious, that our beliefs are based on real data, and that the data that we select/use is the real data. In flux, we often are under pressure to act swiftly. Without time to dig into facts and reason things through, we not only risk forming incorrect conclusions but also risk causing conflict between those who may have drawn different conclusions. The ladder of inference is a rapid-cycle tool that can be used to debrief major decisions:

1.  What do you think happened? Why did it happen?
2.  What questions, if asked, would have led to a different assessment of what happened?

3.   In what ways does this exercise help us better understand how we know what we know?

Learning to unpack our internal sense-making processes is neither easy nor comfortable. Often, we are not aware they exist or how to locate them. The ladder of inference, developed by Harvard Business School professor Chris Argyris (2004) and pictured in Figure 3.3, provides a structured way to reason through those things we either do not remember or subconsciously choose to ignore (the root of our deepest attitudes or deep-seated behaviors). The data are lost to memory, following years of inferential leaps. We come to think of our long-standing assumptions as data, while in reality we may be several steps removed from real data.

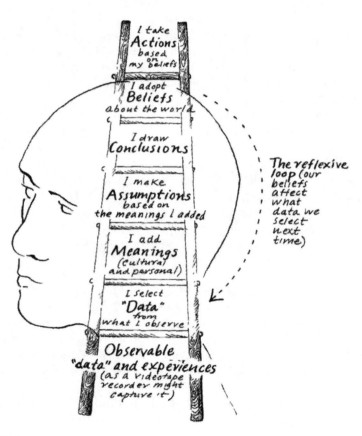

FIGURE 3.3

In leaders' daily practice of layering meaning and drawing conclusions, the ladder of inference positions them to:

1. Ask themselves and their colleagues to become more aware of their own thinking and reasoning through reflection.
2. Make their thinking and reasoning visible to others through advocacy.
3. Interrogate others' thinking and reasoning through inquiry.

The ladder of inference demonstrates the automaticity with which we travel from fact to decision or action. Starting at the bottom rung of the ladder, we have data. From there, we select some portion of the data based on our beliefs and prior experience; we interpret meaning; we apply preexisting assumptions; we draw conclusions based on interpreted facts and our assumptions; we develop beliefs based on these conclusions; and we take actions that seem 'right' because they are based on what we believe.

This series of reflexes can constitute—or at least contribute to—a debilitating and deleterious cycle of beliefs impacting how we view reality. It can lead to neglecting select facts, forming conjured conclusions, missing facts, and skipping steps in the reasoning process. This recognition seeks resolution by or through mutual purpose that takes shape as framed by the fourth learning discipline within a systems mindset, *team learning*.

## Tool 4: Dialogue for Team Learning

At the heart of team learning is a willingness to think, learn, and act together as a living system, engendered by a set of practices designed to get people to do just this—to think, learn, and act together. Not to think alike, but to learn, through effective communication and interaction, to think and act in concert.

Leaders with a systems mindset who guide within nested, tiered systems recognize that, while they may appear independent, they are interdependent, rooted in mutual purpose. This guidance requires continuous deliberation about issues to be addressed, processes to be understood, challenges to be resolved, and redress to be considered: *What has brought us here? What has kept us here? What do we fundamentally believe advances our mutual purpose? What needs to change? What needs to stay the same?*

Leaders with a systems mindset do not mistake agreement for alignment, the latter being the object of team learning, with purposeful arrangement and redesign of scattered elements, orienting lateral and vertical awareness of purpose and current realities. Alignment moves beyond mutual engagement and into the ability to see and respect each other's work, all the while exposing mental models.

Dialogues for team learning to seamlessly integrate into team settings are as follows:

1.  Ask others to 'share and suspend' assumptions and beliefs.
2.  Open with a 'check-in' and close with a 'check-out.'
3.  Make optional or alternate elaborate preparation that might inhibit free conversation.
4.  Encourage and champion co-created agendas.
5.  Facilitate conversation through common meaning, gently bringing people from a frame of agreement/disagreement into alignment with mutual purpose.

## Tool 5: Causal Loop Diagrams

The fifth learning discipline, systems thinking, serves as an underlying philosophy for, and underscores an awareness of, the role structures play in creating and shaping the conditions for adaptive change, while also recognizing that there are powerful components of operating systems of which we are unaware, pulling us toward the realization that there are consequences to our actions to which we may have been oblivious. Systems thinking is, in this sense, a useful constant, a diagnostic, a disciplined approach not only for close examination of root causes but for relational mapping of problems before acting on them. This allows us to ask better questions, rather than to fall back on assumptions and jump to conclusions.

Moving from observation (raw data), to identification (trending behaviors over time), and to recognition or surfacing of underlying structures that drive those events and patterns, systems thinking exposes shifting structures that are not serving us well (including our own mental models) so that we open ourselves up to choices and pathways to grasp a situation more fully and in new and different ways. It is here that we recognize interrelated, often multiple, valid responses, some underappreciated and others unpopular. At the same time, the principles of systems thinking bring into high relief that there are no isolated decisions and solutions: each choice we make impacts other parts of the system. By anticipating and quantifying that impact on shifting structures with each trade-off, we can minimize the severity of risk or even use it to our own advantage.

Causal loops are effective vehicles for identifying, describing, and communicating relationships between component parts of systems and for outlining those relationships to others that are difficult to describe. As an alternative to linear cause-and-effect chains, causal loop diagramming aids in visualizing the ways in which variables in a system are causally interrelated. For more emergent systems, causes of an observed pattern of behavior can be revealed within these feedback structures, and, while there will be elements that are static, change slowly, or are not connected to the problem, others will surface as far more dynamic.

The causal loop diagram (CLD) is a foundational tool used in system dynamics, a method of analysis used to develop an understanding of complex systems that enables leaders to identify and visually display intricate processes and root causes. Jay Forrester of MIT's Sloan School of Management (1961) founded system dynamics in the 1950s with his groundbreaking *Industrial Dynamics*. Decades later, Peter Senge, in *The Fifth Discipline* (2012), used CLD as a centerpiece of systems thinking, the fifth learning discipline. Valuable for telling compelling stories that describe how systems work, the practice of drawing causal loop diagrams forces individuals to draft and develop shared narrative in order to deeply understand a situation: see Figure 3.4.

A system behaves in the manner it does owing to the nature of multitudinous influences, some of which can be changed, others cannot, some can be minimized, and others can be expanded on. A causal loop diagram simulates systematic feedback in processes by showing how one variable affects another, down the variable-to-variable chain of causes and effects. By looking across all known interactions, with the focus shifting from a single interplay between two variables to the entire system, the most effective loops reveal connections or relationships between parts of the organization or system that were heretofore unnoticed.

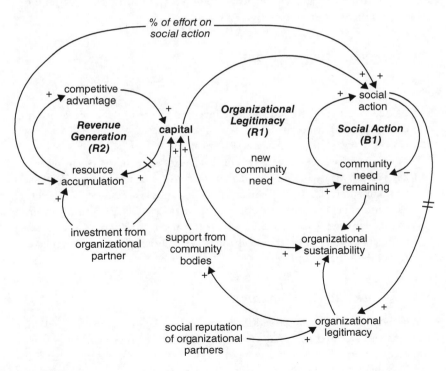

**FIGURE 3.4**

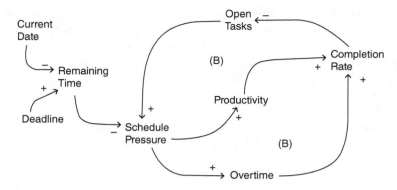

**FIGURE 3.5**

Rather than fixating on whether loops look 'right,' ask yourself whether the loop accurately reflects the story your team has set out to depict. Loops become shorthand for what we perceive as the current state; using that perspective, they are as close to 'right' as they need to be and serve to increase one's ability to deduce and predict systemic behaviors: see Figure 3.5.

## Try Now: Draw Your Own Loops

Select a problem or concern that is accelerating or has recently accelerated.

1. Ask: What three factors do you believe contributed to the acceleration of the problem or concern?
2. Create: Create a loop. This is a *reinforcing* loop.
3. Next, try a *balancing* loop, a system that promotes stability. Begin with one key variable that describes an element that is core to the system. This might be a human, technological, financial, and/or physical resource. What other elements affect that variable? For each element, ask: What is causing changes to this element? What causes it to vary? If you get stuck, work forward: what is the effect when this variable changes? What other elements must change? A sample is shown in Figure 3.6.

## Tool 6: Stock and Flow Diagrams

Stock and flow diagrams provide a richer visual language than causal loop diagrams and are used to define and distinguish between six elements—stocks, flows, converters, connectors, sources, and sinks—to translate a complex situation into mathematical units to specify interrelationships:

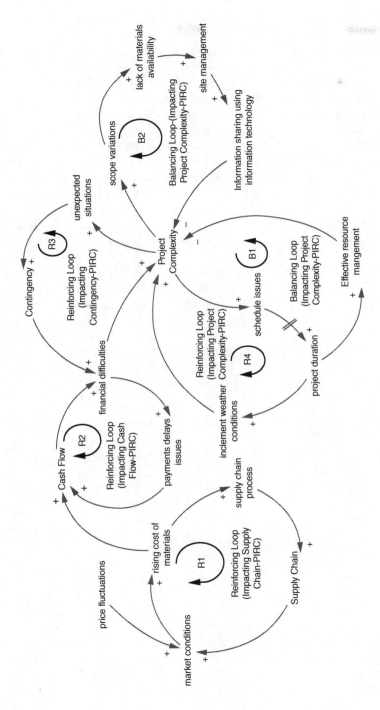

**FIGURE 3.6**

- **Stock:** the accumulation of some quantity, which may or may not feel traditionally measurable (e.g., level of workplace morale)
- **Flow:** the rate at which those quantities flow into a stock (causing it to increase) or out of a stock (causing it to decrease); deciphering flow patterns promotes a better understanding of delays, obstacles, and challenges
- **Converter:** the factor that influences the rate of flow from one stock to another; flows vary; understanding flow patterns can be determinative of system timing
- **Connector:** the interrelationship between stock, flow, and converter is a mathematical formula associated with each that explicitly defines change made possible by another change, revealing how parts of a system influence each other (stocks only by flows; flows by stocks, flows, and converters; converters either not at all or by stocks, flows, and converters)
- **Sources/sinks:** stocks that lie outside the model's boundary, used to show that a stock is either flowing *from a source* or *into a sink* outside the model's boundary

Notation in stock and flow diagrams was originated with Jay Forrester (1961). Based on the flow of water into/out of reservoirs, the key feature is that each construct can be specified using a mathematical formula. Viewed in this way, such fully specified models enable visualization in a corresponding set of integral equations. Stock and flow models can recreate, through simulation, models of just about any complex issue by reproducing inflows and outflows (see Figure 3.7). This sparks questions such as: What is accumulating? What is causing the increase? What might lead to a decrease?

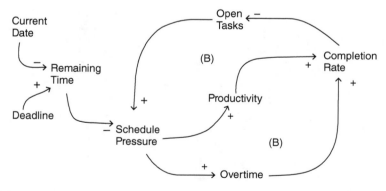

**FIGURE 3.7**

Sort diagrammatic parts according to the categories identified in Figure 3.8. Make your thinking explicit.

Every arrow is linked to a formula, embodying collective commentary not just about assumptions underlying a given relationship but on the way each element influences others: See Figure 3.9.

| PART | CATEGORY | COMMENT |
|---|---|---|
| Open tasks | Stock | The number of open tasks must be stock - on any given day - we cannot know how many open tasks remain without either explicitly counting them or explicitly keeping track of our progress. |
| Completion rate | Flow | The completion rate is the only element that has a direct impact on stock. |
| Deadline | Converter (Boundary value) | The deadline is a boundary value because it is not set from the outside. We represent these kinds of values using converters that have no further inputs. |
| Current date | Converter (Boundary value) | The current date is also a boundary value, albeit not a constant one. |
| Remaining time | Converter | It is an auxiliary that can be derived from the current date and the deadline. |
| Schedule pressure | Converter | The schedule pressure can be calculated at any given time, the remaining time and the number of open tasks. |
| Productivity & overtime | Converter | Productivity and overtime are conceptually harder to model that the other elements. To keep our model simple initially, we assume that my current productivity only depends on the current schedule pressure and not on my past behavior. We make the same assumption about the overtime (i.e., the normal workday plus overtime) I work. |

FIGURE 3.8

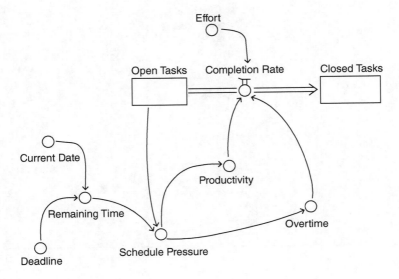

FIGURE 3.9

## Tool 7: The Iceberg

The iceberg is a systems thinking tool designed to help an individual or team discover patterns of behavior, supporting structures, and mental models that underlie a particular event.

Designed to help differentiate between the 'seen' (often exceedingly little) and the 'unseen' (a massive amount), the iceberg illustrates the levels of abstraction to a situation or organization, from observable *events*, to underlying *patterns* that generate those events, to supporting *structures*, and ultimately to *mental models* used to inform those structures, all to inform and expand on one's perception of a situation in context (see Figure 3.10).

Leveraging the iceberg helps organizations routinely describe and solve problems through multiple lenses: as *events*, as *patterns* or *trends*, and as *structures* producing those patterns or trends. When tackling a complex challenge, using the

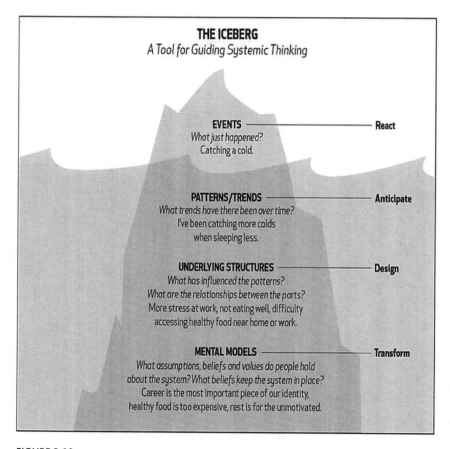

### THE ICEBERG
#### A Tool for Guiding Systemic Thinking

**EVENTS** ——————————— **React**
What just happened?
Catching a cold.

**PATTERNS/TRENDS** ——————————— **Anticipate**
What trends have there been over time?
I've been catching more colds
when sleeping less.

**UNDERLYING STRUCTURES** ——————————— **Design**
What has influenced the patterns?
What are the relationships between the parts?
More stress at work, not eating well, difficulty
accessing healthy food near home or work.

**MENTAL MODELS** ——————————— **Transform**
What assumptions, beliefs and values do people hold
about the system? What beliefs keep the system in place?
Career is the most important piece of our identity,
healthy food is too expensive, rest is for the unmotivated.

**FIGURE 3.10**

iceberg enables the pairing of a high-level view with ground-level insights from those directly addressing the challenge, stretching people just out of daily operational comfort zones to see things differently without stretching so far as to be unrelatable.

When addressing a pressing problem, a systems mindset assumes that approximately 90% of an iceberg is underwater. And the width of the iceberg is nearly 30% larger than what you can see on the surface. With this logic—that what exists underwater creates the 'seen behavior' (what exists above the surface)—a systems mindset resists creating solutions based on a single event or as a temporary fix, which often leads to a repeat of the problem. The iceberg model's four-step approach to evaluating a problem allows identification of the root causes, underlying structures, and mental models that trigger problematic events. Honoring diverse and even divergent perspectives and views is key to holistically conceived evidence-based solutions. Whether you are ready to start now or are looking to build up to it, the preceding set of tools combined with the practices below will help shift your approach to, and help you adopt, a systems mindset.

## Systems Mindset Practices

### Try Today

1.  Record two things, side by side, as they refer to a complex problem: first, your personal vision for solving it (the results you most want to see); and second, a realistic assessment of what is. Take note of bridges and gaps.
2.  Form a 'systems team' around this complex problem and enable, through formal structures, cross-function and interdepartmental group interaction.
3.  Allocate team time to break problems down into component parts through facilitated mapping practices.
4.  Read or reread about root cause analysis through the *Five Whys* (Serrat, 2017), a problem-solving method that explores the underlying cause and effect of particular problems. The primary goal is to determine the root cause of a defect or a problem by successively asking the question "Why?"

### Build a Weekly Practice

1.  Dedicate time in meetings to explicit cross-organizations connection points.
2.  Interrogate the systems around you. Work two questions into each team meeting: *What do you want to be true that isn't true now? What is stopping that truth from being realized?*
3.  Work through the evolution of a complex problem using Senge's framework of five learning disciplines (personal mastery, shared vision, mental models, team learning, systems thinking).

4. Study analogous systems and reinforce structural couplings as understood via logic modeling, causal loop, and/or stock and flow.
5. Use systems thinking to identify root causes and human-centered design to rapidly prototype and test solutions, affording the opportunity to continuously shed light on root causes and uncover new opportunities to customize.
6. Actively ask of any organizational system, thereby shifting from *problem to possibility*: *What are the elements? How are they connected? How do they create the result we are seeing?*

## *Try Monthly*

1. Create new vehicles and/or spaces for asking questions that get underneath interdependency and change through the three iceberg lenses (event, pattern/trend, structure).
2. Routinely pose big-picture questions that are proposed/fielded equitably for all staff to discuss. Evince horizontal generative dialogues around shared practices, processes, and values.
3. Form a 'systems team' to present a problem of practice using one of the seven tools, rotate monthly, and share out discoveries at cross-departmental meetings.
4. Think holistically. Observe the system and seek to understand relational parts of the system *through and with* those who constitute the system.
5. Establish and center mutual purpose and shared values. Center the question: In what ways does current organizational culture reinforce/promote or does it hinder/deny mutual purpose and shared values?

# 4
# ENTREPRENEURIAL MINDSET

I have not failed, I've just found 10,000 ways that won't work.

—*Thomas Edison*

## What Is an Entrepreneurial Mindset?

The dual-cylinder nature of entrepreneurship—massive global growth in engagements in entrepreneurial pursuits (extensive course and degree program development has made entrepreneurship one of the fastest growing areas of undergraduate study; Torrance & Rauch, 2013) reveals entrepreneurship's concurrent and complementary meteoric rise in the workplace and on campus.

In the 1980s, college courses in entrepreneurship began to materialize on university rosters, across approximately 250 campuses. By 2008, the number of university courses had grown to over 5,000 (Guilles, 2015). By 2013, over 400,000 students were enrolled in entrepreneurship courses, with 9,000 faculty members instructing in the subject area (Torrance & Rauch, 2013). From 2017 to 2021, undergraduate entrepreneurship program offerings increased by nearly 24%, demonstrating continued curricular expansion in response to market demand (Mescon & van Rest, 2021).

Even with this explosive growth, there is still debate over whether 'being entrepreneurial' is something people are born with or something that can be learned. This very question became the basis for scholarship on the set of traits, motivations, attitudes, behaviors, and actions that contribute to entrepreneurial

DOI: 10.4324/b23253-5

activity (typically conceived of as launching or founding a new venture, although not necessarily leading to that), entrepreneurial intentions, and entrepreneurial orientation, reconceived and described herein as an entrepreneurial mindset.

Entrepreneurial thinking is described in the business literature and, more specifically, in management theory as *the ability to recognize and leverage opportunity (to introduce new goods or services) within uncertain and unpredictable environments*. Early attempts to isolate elements of entrepreneurial thinking that had a direct relationship to new venture creation were inconclusive, and the lack of a coherent conceptual framework for entrepreneurship enabled default to individual components—characteristics of entrepreneurs, opportunity recognition, resource acquisition—with less consideration as to whether any component part offers explanatory power for or is related to the others. Early modeling of the 'entrepreneurial process' included an individual's identification and evaluation of opportunity, the decision whether to exploit it, efforts to obtain resources, organizing those resources in new ways, and strategic planning approaches for the new venture: see Figure 4.1.

The model, of course, requires and relies on people acting on data, making the decision to 'act entrepreneurially' or, said another way, to practice entrepreneurship. A broad mix of psychological factors—personality traits, motives, cognitive characteristics, skills—have been studied to identify and measure specific constructs of entrepreneurial thinking and their relationships to entrepreneurial practice. As researchers set out to develop what ultimately led to a comprehensive measure for the constellation of motives, skills, and traits that distinguish entrepreneurs from non-entrepreneurs and contribute to entrepreneurial success, there emerged a progressively sophisticated understanding of how those

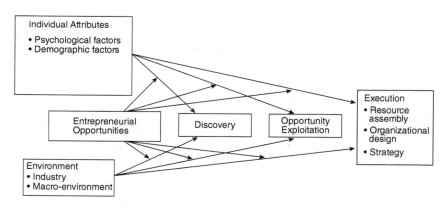

**FIGURE 4.1**

traits, motives, characteristics, and skills work together to capture what came to be known as the entrepreneurial mindset (EM).

A century ago, the publication of Frank Knight's *Risk, Uncertainty and Profit* (1921) marked a key launch point into rigorous research on the personalities of entrepreneurs that set them apart from general business managers. In the decades that followed, research continued to investigate specific individual traits that prompted people to become entrepreneurs, as well as personal motivations and preferences that kept entrepreneurs on their chosen path. These studies were conducted in high-growth sectors, often supported by venture capital (VC), where entrepreneurs faced a high probability of business failure, a low probability of positive outcomes, and nominal average return.

Between 1970 and 2000, the five-factor model (FFM) of personality became a theoretical frame for understanding how specific traits—need for achievement, locus of control, self-efficacy, innovativeness, tolerance of uncertainty—exert influence over entrepreneurial outcomes via a series of pathways that act as conduits for FFM's broader "macro traits":

1. **Openness to experience:** breadth, depth, originality, and complexity of an individual's mental and experimental life
2. **Conscientiousness:** socially prescribed impulse control that facilitates task- and goal-oriented behavior
3. **Extraversion:** an energetic approach toward the social and material world; includes sociability, activity, and assertiveness
4. **Agreeableness:** contrasts a prosocial and communal orientation toward others with antagonism; includes altruism, tendermindedness, trust, modesty
5. **Emotional stability:** contrasts even-temperedness with negative emotionality, such as feeling anxious, nervous, sad, tense

While the 'Big-5' provided an organizing structure for examining the relationship between personality traits and entrepreneurial thinking and doing, its overly general nature and macro personality traits did not accurately predict situational behaviors of entrepreneurs, such that understanding a person's Big-5 personality did not deepen one's understanding of specific mechanisms through which personality impacts entrepreneurial attitudes and actions (Kanfer, 1992; Rauch, 2014). With the limitations of the Big-5 framework to describe a coherent portrait of the entrepreneur, researchers shifted and created a multidimensional personality framework that incorporates other qualities such as self-efficacy, innovativeness, locus of control, and need for achievement.

Researchers began to test sets of individual characteristics in the development of a comprehensive instrument to measure the entrepreneurial mindset. In search of a more systematic and comprehensive approach to measuring the facets of EM and its relationship to entrepreneurial actions, a handful of instruments (all of which attempt to measure individual traits and motives that characterize entrepreneurs) were designed:

1. The general enterprising tendency test (Caird, 2013) measures five facets of the entrepreneurial individual: need for achievement, autonomy, creative tendency, calculated risk-taking, and internal locus of control. Evidence suggests that entrepreneurs score higher on each dimension than control groups.
2. The entrepreneurial attitude scale (EAS; Robinson et al., 1991) assesses four constructs: need for achievement, self-esteem, personal control, and innovation. Hailed as an attitudinal measure rather than a personality measure, several items strongly resemble those on personality instruments. Entrepreneurs scored higher than managers on all four dimensions.
3. The measure of entrepreneurial tendencies and abilities (META; Leutner et al., 2014) examines four constructs: entrepreneurial awareness, entrepreneurial creativity, opportunism, and vision. Scores on these dimensions are positively associated with self-reported entrepreneurial achievement and activities.
4. The Entrepreneurship Mindset Profile, or EMP™ (www.emindsetprofile.com/icf/): Considering the development and use of the tools above, a team of researchers at Eckerd College's Center for Creative Leadership set out to identify a comprehensive list of dimensions that characterize entrepreneurs and contribute to entrepreneurial success to help leaders, students, and entrepreneurs assess the degree to which they are using an EM, or traits and skills unique to entrepreneurs.

This approach differed from past efforts in its (four-part) focus:

1. Traits and motivations of entrepreneurial individuals
2. Characteristics of entrepreneurial organizations
3. Creativity and innovation (rather than entrepreneurial activity per se)
4. Direct conversations with entrepreneurs; specifically, soliciting entrepreneurs' views on characteristics that most distinguished them from non-entrepreneurs

Moving away from broader domains and toward more specific skills and traits confirmed the hypotheses among researchers that they yielded more meaningful associations with entrepreneurial outcomes (Zhao et al., 2010), while exclusive focus on broader domains underestimated the association between personality and entrepreneurial outcomes.

The ability to link specific traits that are highly correlated with entrepreneurial outcomes became part of the design frame for measuring EM Key to the design approach was the recognition that developing a tool to measure EM using defining characteristics of 'thinking entrepreneurially' must also consider contextual factors such as resource scarcity and high uncertainty and, with this, the ability to experiment, or quickly sense, take action, and organize under scarce, uncertain conditions.

*Dimensions Making Up the EMP*

Traits

Independence: The desire to work with a high degree of independence (e.g., *I'm uncomfortable when expected to follow others' rules*).

Preference for Limited Structure: A preference for tasks and situations with little formal structure (e.g., *I find it boring to work on clearly structured tasks*).

Nonconformity: A preference for acting in unique ways; an interest in being perceived as unique (e.g., *I like to stand out from the crowd*).

Risk Acceptance: A willingness to pursue an idea or a desired goal even when the probability of succeeding is low (e.g., *I'm willing to take a certain amount of risk to achieve real success*).

Action Orientation: A tendency to show initiative, make decisions quickly. and feel impatient for results (e.g., *I tend to make decisions quickly*).

Passion: A tendency to experience one's work as exciting and enjoyable rather than tedious and draining (e.g., *I'm passionate about the work that I do*).

Need to Achieve: The desire to achieve at a high level (e.g., *I want to be the best at what I do*).

Skills

Future Focus: The ability to think beyond the immediate situation and plan for the future (e.g., *I'm focused on the long term*).

Idea Generation: The ability to generate multiple and novel ideas and to find multiple approaches for achieving goals (e.g., *Sometimes the ideas just bubble out of me*).

Execution: The ability to turn ideas into actionable plans; the ability to implement ideas well (e.g., *I have a reputation for being able to take an idea and make it work*).

Self-Confidence: A general belief in one's ability to leverage skills and talents to achieve important goals (e.g., *I am a self-confident person*).

Optimism: The ability to maintain a generally positive attitude about various aspects of one's life and the world (e.g., *Even when things aren't going well, I look on the bright side*).

Persistence: The ability to bounce back quickly from disappointment and to remain persistent in the face of setbacks (e.g., *I do not give up easily*).

Interpersonal Sensitivity: A high level of sensitivity to and concern for the well-being of those with whom one works (e.g., *I'm sensitive to others' feelings*).

**FIGURE 4.2**

The resulting distinction between dimensions that are 'personality-like' (those traits and motivations that are relatively enduring) and those considered 'skills' (more readily developable) warrants less professional attention paid to activation of the more stable dimensions associated with entrepreneurial outcomes (e.g., achievement motivation, nonconformity) than to those that are more malleable (e.g., self-confidence, persistence, execution). The latter set is comprised of ideal candidates for development in the workplace. See Figure 4.2.

## Why Do Leaders Need an Entrepreneurial Mindset?

Entrepreneurship sparks innovation, drives employment, fuels economic development, and offers solutions to environmental, social, and societal challenges. For any of entrepreneurship's sparks and drivers to ignite, the catalytic entrepreneurial mindset enables recognition and activation of opportunities, make decisions with limited information, embrace change, and remain resilient in uncertain, complex conditions.

Leaders who practice an entrepreneurial mindset are not only resourceful, action-oriented, and highly engaged, but they also possess optimistic interpretations of adverse events, see problems as potential opportunities, and possess a core understanding that pursuit and follow-through lead to further unforeseen opportunities. With flux comes competing priorities, cascading opportunities, limited resources, erratic market conditions, and uncertain capacity, all demanding ambidextrousness. Helping leaders to do this, the entrepreneurial mindset relies on three habits: creativity, improvisation, and self-leadership.

Creativity, which is difficult to classify owing to its diffuseness and broad application to a wide range of processes and people, is the capacity to produce new ideas, insights, inventions, products, or objects that are considered to be unique, useful, and of value to others (Neck, 2010). For leaders, the importance of creativity to navigate the unknown involves 'whole-brain' thinking and doing (Pink, 2006), seamlessly integrating what has been called (though not scientifically supported) left-brain thinking (e.g., logic, analysis) with right-brain thinking (e.g., spatial relations, emotion, synthesis).

Highly creative individuals have been found to possess dialectic personalities and operate not in polarized ways (e.g., disciplined vs. playful, conventional vs. radical) but instead at *both* poles (Csikszentmihalyi, 1996). Leaders with an entrepreneurial mindset then can be both optimistic and pragmatic, can envision success while also preparing for failure, are autonomous and committed to the organization.

Improvisation—the art of spontaneous creation without preparation—is the second key leadership habit of an entrepreneurial mindset. While improvisation may evoke for many people the act of performing under pressure, leading through flux translates into improvisation as the ability to function, remain acutely present in the moment, and act. In this sense, the habit of improvisation builds a leader's natural inclination to confront the unexpected. Self-leadership, a process whereby leaders use behavior-focused strategies, natural rewards, and constructive thought patterns to build the necessary motivation to lead in and through new directions, seek out innovations, and build new ventures, is the third habit honed through an entrepreneurial mindset.

Behavior-focused strategies—self-observation, goal setting, self-cueing, self-reward, self-correction—are methods to increase awareness, particularly through challenging times, of how, when, and why we behave the way we do in certain circumstances. Natural rewards make a task or activity more enjoyable by building in certain features or reshaping perceptions to focus on its most positive aspects and the value it holds. Constructive thought patterns help leaders form productive ways of thinking that benefit individual and team performance.

## Learning Frames and Activations for an Entrepreneurial Mindset

### Tool 1: Entrepreneurial Mindset Profile

The Entrepreneurial Mindset Profile (EMP) was developed by a team of psychologists and researchers at the Eckerd College Leadership Development Institute, an affiliate of the Center for Creative Leadership, to measure a set of validated constructs that differentiates entrepreneurs from non-entrepreneurs. Originally developed for use with corporate leaders, the EMP has since been used in coaching with organizational teams, with students, and with self-identified entrepreneurs and aspiring entrepreneurs. The tool offers additional insight into one's unique profile of entrepreneurial strengths, and team/group reports used in conjunction with individual reports help leaders to better understand and leverage their individual and collective assets for complementary team building.

Practicing an entrepreneurial mindset invites leaders to consistently: (a) consider ways to enhance one or more elements of entrepreneurial thought and action and (b) actively seek out ways to identify and leverage the entrepreneurial skills and traits as measured by the EMP (interpersonal sensitivity, independence, risk tolerance, persistence, execution, passion, preference for limited structure, action orientation, need to achieve, future focus, idea generation, self-confidence, optimism, nonconformity).

When using the EMP, leaders are cautioned to focus on development as opposed to selection. Given the face validity of the items, individuals could manipulate their response, and until and unless the EMP proves to have predictive validity in hiring decisions, it is useful for selecting from among existing trait and skill pools those best suited for complementary versus oppositional roles on project teams, with scale mapping to discrete projects.

Review EMP scores with a critical eye toward one's organizational role and function and parlay results into complementary skill/trait project teams. For example, staff and distribute core project teams by using a score threshold assigned to select EMP dimensions, by task. For a strategic planning process, scales might be mapped like this: (1.) overall design of strategic plan/formation of pillars: future focus, idea generation; (2.) alignment of organizational objectives with strategic plan pillars: optimism, interpersonal sensitivity; (3.) manage plan implementation/develop tactics: action orientation, execution.

## Tool 2: Storyboard

Storyboarding is a form of prototyping that provides a high-level view of thoughts and ideas arranged in sequence in the form of drawings, sketches, or illustrations. Storyboarding was developed in the 1930s by Walt Disney animator Webb Smith, who pinned up sketches of scenes in order to visualize scenes and target issues or inconsistencies before going into production. Since then, storyboarding has become a business tool for creating a deeper understanding of how the product or service interacts with the primary beneficiary: see Figure 4.3.

The idea is to literally illustrate a richer understanding of the problem the stakeholder is experiencing, the offer, or solution, to that problem, and the way/s in which the customer benefits from the solution. There is deep value in story,

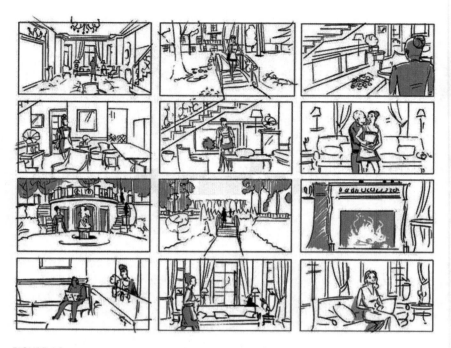

**FIGURE 4.3**

and the storyboard places the beneficiary at the center. A common structure for a storyboard is the three-part problem–solution–benefit framework:

1. What is the problem the [client/customer/employee/stakeholder] is experiencing?
2. What are we offering as a solution to the problem?
3. How will the [client/customer/employee/stakeholder] benefit from the solution?

Develop an action experiment for each question; be specific: What is the question the experiment is designed to examine? What is your hypothesis? Conduct the action experiment. What did you learn? What surprised you? What did you confirm? How will you build your learnings into the next experiment? Is your original design different than you originally imagined? If so, how so?

### Tool 3: Team, Resources, Idea, Market (TRIM)

TRIM is a planning tool that streamlines four areas of entrepreneurial planning (see Table 4.1). First, it helps leaders to identify skill types, goal orientations, and roles for a particular project. Second, it helps leaders to locate the resources that are needed versus those that are available for the project. Third, it elucidates

**TABLE 4.1** TRIM

| Team | Resources |
|---|---|
| Who needs to be on the project from the start?<br>How will you recruit them?<br>What skills/traits (from the EMP) does each person bring to the team?<br>What types of work experiences are related to the idea?<br>What networks does each person bring to the idea?<br>Are the project-related goals for each team member aligned?<br>What are the roles of each team member?<br>How will project tasks/ownership be distributed? | What [human/financial/tech/physical] resources do you currently have that you can use to get started?<br>If resources are limited, can you still get started?<br>What resources will you need to continue? Are these resources able to be secured? |
| **Idea** | **Market** |
| What is the clearest and simplest way to describe the idea?<br>How is the idea unique or differentiated from others in the market?<br>What problem is the idea solving?<br>What market trends support the idea solving this problem?<br>What is the primary benefit(/value proposition)? | What are the three primary markets?<br>What does each market care most about?<br>How will you reach your markets (through which channels)?<br>What is the approximate size of each market?<br>Willingness to pay? |

for leaders the finer details of the project idea. Finally, it helps leaders to outline the potential market(s). TRIM not only lends clarity in these four areas but also promotes thinking through the connectivity between quadrants and the rationale behind pairing discrete skills and traits evidenced by the EMP for a particular project.

## Tool 4: Failure Résumé

'Fear of failure' has been characterized as an emotional, cognitive and behavioral reaction to the negative consequences one anticipates for failing to achieve a goal. Why? First, it is embarrassing. Second, we imagine that we will let people (including ourselves) down. Failure is linked to our sense of self-worth. After repeated failures, if negative/less-than thoughts begin to infiltrate and settle in, this could result in us either not fully trying to reach our goals or significantly lowering our standards of success, as not pursuing an important goal feels less painful than finding out that we are *not competent enough* to achieve it.

No matter the root and no matter the consequences, leaders with an entrepreneurial mindset foreground failure as inevitable and that it can and should be embraced. In the moments immediately following a failure, we often do not reflect on it. Our colleague, Angela Duckworth, in *Grit: The Power of Passion and Perseverance* (2016), found that those who were highly successful were unusually resilient and hardworking, and that grit explains why, when confronted with the possibility of failure, some redouble efforts while others head straight for the door.

When individuals were asked to identify with statements such as "Setbacks don't discourage me," "I don't give up easily," and "My interests change from year to year," grit was a reliable predictor of who made it through and who did not. This embracing of the high possibility of failure differentiated those individuals who made it through a physically and mentally demanding regime and failed as many times as the dropouts, but did not allow those failures to define them and were able to quickly remind themselves that they are imperfect human beings and learn from their mistakes

With grit, failure is not something to fear, but rather something that we can overcome and grow from. According to Duckworth, we should embrace it as a necessary part of success. Rather than "I failed; I'm going to get back up and be resilient," a failure résumé puts in front of us "Why did I fail? What should I do so that I am less likely to fail next time, which is when I am going to get up again and do it." Grit is the flipside of resilience, not only in the face of failure but through perseverance and adherence to one's long-term goals. Duckworth's examination of the relationship between grit and high achievement led to the ascertaining of the qualities most predictive of persistence in highly challenging situations.

In the spirit of building attributes that comprise grit, create a failure résumé. Duckworth's work has been widely taken up in school reform circles as a way of thinking about building students' non-cognitive skills, critical for later life success. There have been detractors, with the most prominent critique being that an emphasis on grit is a way to "blame the victim" rather than take up larger questions of social, economic, and racial justice. If only the most disadvantaged were grittier, they could overcome serious challenges. Schools and families focus on the variables they can control and thus see students' abilities to persevere and respond to adversity as critical to their success. This focus on grit lends an impoverished view of human motivation—that, in the long term, people do not persevere at things because they are good at persevering, but rather they persevere because they find things worth investing in. The implication for schools is that they should spend less time trying to locate and magnify students' grit, and more time thinking about how their offerings could help students develop purpose and passion.

## Build a Failure Résumé

Outline what you consider to be five of your 'biggest fails'—academic, professional, or social. For each, describe what you learned and what others learned from you. Share your résumé with at least one other member of your team. Compare your learnings rather than the list of self-professed failures.

## Tool 5: Observations to Insights

Observation is a core tenet of design thinking, a human-centered approach to design anchored in customer needs, rapid prototyping, and idea generation. First, identify an area of high interest for you. Next, find a space to observe related to this area. What is most important is that you observe people. Design thinking is human-centered, and desirability is central. The simple act of deeply observing people will lead to insights as to what they need and to becoming increasingly comfortable with *seeing with purpose*, with building intentional insights about people, and differentiating observing from seeing.

Observe for 60–90 minutes. Closely monitor behaviors, habits, and activities of potential users, customers, clients, or participants *in their own environment*. Record notes using a table such as Table 4.2 to help you to organize your thoughts. Develop keen observation skills by practicing the AEIOU framework's five dimensions of observation. In the AEIOU framework, which aspect of observation did you find most useful? Most challenging? What insight can you identify for the space you observed? Does your insight represent a need or a solution?

## Tool 6: Empathy Map

Develop a fuller understanding of your customer is the focal point of user experience (UX) design. To truly understand the user's thought process and needs, it is important to empathize with them. Empathy mapping of a particular persona or target customer/user is a succinct and visual depiction of voices, including and

**TABLE 4.2** Observation Skills Development Worksheet

Activities (A.): What are people doing?

Environment (E.): How are people using
the environment? What's the role of the
environment?

Interactions (I.): What routines do
you notice? Do you observe special
interactions between people? Between
people and objects?

Objects (O.): What objects are being used,
what objects are being left alone? How
are people engaging with objects?

Users/participants (U.): Who are they, and
what are their roles?

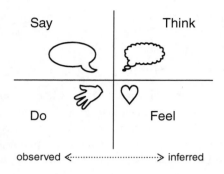

**FIGURE 4.4**

especially struggles and frustrations. An empathy map is an easy-to-digest visual showing group emotions, amalgamation of observations, and gauging of actionable insights. The typical basic map contains four quadrants: *say* (records what users say about the product or service during interviews or testing sessions; *think* (discovering what users think—and often do not communicate—when interacting with a product or service); *do* (user actions/typical behaviors); and *feel* (users' emotional state and fluctuations throughout their interactions with the product or service); see Figure 4.4.

## Entrepreneurial Mindset Practices

### Try Today

1. Administer the EMP™ to assess the entrepreneurial capacity of team members and to help individuals and teams understand the concept of EM as well as their own unique profiles.
2. Take one idea and draw it in action (problem → solution → benefit or outcome); write down three preliminary foundational questions you have.

### Build a Weekly Practice

1. Promote activities that enhance entrepreneurial skills and develop entrepreneurial traits, prioritizing development over 'rightness.'
2. Establish a climate in which learning through failure is encouraged and celebrated.
3. Build entrepreneurial 'habits'—start small (so small that you cannot say no; sufficiently easy to take on without great motivation); increase your activity in very small ways; gradually build your activity to keep momentum; break it into smaller chunks; plan to fail.

## *Try Monthly*

1. Identify skills or traits on the EMP™ with a critical eye toward one's role within the organization and parlay results into complementary skill/trait project teams.
2. Consider organization-wide skills or traits that may be underdeveloped and outline a growth goal for each area.
3. Publicly acknowledge project teams' application of one or more EMP™ skills or traits.
4. Structure projects that underscore resilience, or strength, as recovery from perceived failure.
5. Design business processes and practices that invite the courage to fail rather than instill a fear of failure.

# 5

# EQUITY MINDSET

When you are laboring for others let it be with the same zeal as if it were for yourself.

—*Confucius*

## What Is an Equity Mindset?

Equity is a central conversation across sectors, fields, industries, and types of businesses and organizations globally. Systemic inequities exposed and exacerbated worldwide by the pandemic, coupled with intensified (inter)national dialogue on racial injustice and gender disparity, have surfaced systems issues that leaders and organizations have heard about through whisper networks or have seen mounting for years.

Leaders with an equity mindset do their homework on these macro social issues to understand how they impact the micro contexts of companies and teams; they examine unequal outcomes to identify patterns based on race, gender, sexual identity/orientation, citizenship status, and disability, working to remedy inequitable patterns and processes and to improve norms, policies, and dynamics through training for organization-wide learning and improvement. Most organizations lack the skills, frames, and approaches necessary to chart and achieve cultural and inclusive excellence.

Leaders with an **equity mindset** prioritize individual, team, and organizational equity in policies, norms, behavior, and values, operationalized through creating the conditions for personal and team reflection, relational accountability, and systemic sensemaking in norms and communication. They work to ensure

DOI: 10.4324/b23253-6

a diverse workforce and equitable workplace that foster inclusion, psychological safety, authenticity, and belonging.

As Forbes council member Lee Meadows (2020) offers, "Equity is a mindset that, when intertwined with the organizational culture, allows organizational members to see interactions through a broader, talent-based lens. ... The equity mindset is created through a series of focused actions" (2020). An equity mindset drives how leaders enact the vision and values of fairness and humanization; it is horizontalized across the flux mindsets.

So, what are some of the barriers to achieving cultural and inclusive excellence in organizations around the world right now? Leaders share concerns that 'diversity' itself is hotly politicized, which undergirds many presenting workplace issues. Like the child who is an 'identified patient' in a family system—whose supposed bad behavior is cited as the catalyst for therapy, only to be given feedback that it is the family system hurting the child and causing dynamic issues—employees who call out workplace bias and discrimination are typically framed as 'the problem' when, in reality, they are helping leaders to diagnose the problem, lighting a pathway to organizational bravery and equity accountability, often at risk to themselves.

Workplace dynamics can be toxic in ways that purposefully remain off managers' and supervisors' radars through a process commonly referred to as 'managing up.' Leaders with an equity mindset shift from the dominant scarcity logic to an abundance logic, viewing everyone's voice as valuable and each person as part of organizational improvement. This connects them to people and people to each other through building relational accountability, identity-based stress navigation and self-care skills, and equitable communication norms. Understanding people's lived realities and listening to their stories matter to these processes. These help leaders to identify and transcend old 'managing up' mentalities.

Let us define key terms related to workplace equity. **Equality** provides access to the same resources and opportunities across employees, regardless of preexisting barriers; it assumes all people have access to the same advantages and opportunities. Equality is aspirational; equity is actionable. **Equity** is the absence of systematic disparities between groups with differing levels of underlying social advantage and disadvantage. Equity requires differentiating access to resources and opportunities based on existing identity-based privileges and disadvantages. Equity addresses systemic inequity, understanding that individuals have differential access to resources and opportunities and distributing resources accordingly to achieve equal results. Institutionalizing equity means developing and institutionalizing policies and procedures that counterbalance varying degrees of advantage and creating expectations and accountability for being just and inclusive in behavior in and beyond teams.

**Diversity** describes the process of actively bringing together people who have individual (e.g., life experiences, learning styles, personality types) and group (e.g., gender, race, socio-economic status, sexual orientation, nationality) differences. **Inclusion** incorporates different ways of viewing and approaching problems, bringing a range of identities and experiences to the center to drive and achieve excellence. Diversity in the workplace focuses on relationships and treatment between individuals—how people interact and behave—to create a culture in which all voices are invited, people share and take in ideas, and organizational goals reinforce shared understanding that everyone brings value.

**Belonging** is the intersection of diversity, equity, and inclusion and is connected to people's well-being and productivity in an organization, centering people and creating the conditions for them to fully engage and thrive. Belonging is built within a workplace climate that welcomes all voices and encourages people to listen to understand one another's lived experiences. Employees with a heightened sense of belonging more strongly align with equity, support colleagues, and work to create stronger teams. The success of an organization requires that each person feels valued and that they belong. Research shows that diverse teams that actively value and draw on their diversity are more productive and innovative. As well, teammates with a strong sense of belonging are more apt to be resilient, energized, open to change, and trusting of leadership to have their best interest at heart.

*Resource-oriented capacity building* must drive the equity remit. Capacity refers to people's competencies and skills. For organizations and teams, capacity building means offering differentiated professional development that is leveled and that offers a range of professional supports that foster new skills, knowledge, motivation, and inspiration for professional learning that builds resources for individuals and teams to be maximally effective. Equity-oriented capacity building builds shared learning and reciprocal accountability. Accountability is vital to equitable teams, and, thus, sharing accountability for the success of workplace DEI is vital. This informs professional development and training foci and processes.

*Resource-oriented capacity building* illuminates the need for leaders to acknowledge, focus on, and work directly from the existing resources, knowledges, and perspectives people bring to teams, rather than viewing what people do not yet known as deficiency. A humanizing approach to workplace equity work understands it as an adaptive challenge, viewing capacity building through a resource orientation and honoring the capacity that already exists (including understanding how to assess and address its unevenness).

Each person brings their own 'wisdom of practice' (Shulman & Wilson, 2004), and everyone is an expert of their own experience (Ravitch & Carl, 2021). This is an epistemological stance on knowledge, on who is a knower and what constitutes valid knowledge. Thought leader Adrienne Maree Brown (2017) offers this generative insight:

> Liberated relationships are one of the ways we actually create abundant justice, the understanding that there is enough attention, care, resource,

and connection for all of us to access belonging, to be in our dignity, and to be safe in community.

Her words embody an assets-based and human-centered approach to organizational equity work. Approaching equity-focused capacity building as integrated, resource-oriented professional development is a necessary and important organizational position in these times. Setting the tone for resource-oriented capacity building starts with *you*, the lead learner.

## Why Do Leaders and Organizations Need an Equity Mindset?

Despite plentiful corporate DEI initiatives, diversity and inclusion scorecards, and pronouncements about anti-discrimination policies and bias reporting structures, companies and all kinds of organizations continue to lose talent because equity issues are not treated as adaptive challenges (and opportunities), leaders are not fully committed to equity, and the workplace environment is not welcoming or inclusive.

The benefits of a diverse and inclusive workforce are well documented, including increased engagement and productivity, improved financial performance and outputs, and reduced turnover. A recent poll conducted by JUST Capital and the Harris Poll reports that 79% of U.S. employees believe it is important for companies to promote workplace racial diversity and equity; 64% feel they should do more to promote equity; 95% of Black Americans believe companies should promote racial equality; and 80% believe they can do more.

Importantly, equity and DEI are not synonymous; DEI is the current name given to approaches that seek to achieve organizational equity, largely through raising awareness. DEI looks quite similar across sectors and quite different across country contexts and continents, which has significant implications for how global businesses and organizations must consider and approach equity across country contexts. In the United States, the major entry point for workplace DEI is race, with a subset focus on culture in training and conversations about equity, bias, and identity. In Europe, priority DEI entry points are gender inequality and social class/caste. That entry points for workplace DEI are so contextual illuminates that national context must be considered in terms of the overall approach, focus, and design of equity work. Across contexts, the equity function should be aligned through strong boundary spanning so that learning integrates and informs widely; sadly, it rarely is.

To state historical fact, the majority of U.S. and European institutions were built by and for White male populations. We need not judge this; it is historical fact. More important to current workplace equity is that organizations have not been innovated past this early mindset and model in significant ways since their institutionalization. Embedded artifacts of this old work model include compliance-based rather than learning-oriented workplace communications and policies, inequitable communication norms, and biased evaluations of professionalism based on normative White male behavior standards. These are artifacts of a time long gone that no longer reflect many workforce realities.

Structural biases are embedded in workplace logics, policies, processes, physical spaces, communication norms and team dynamics, management ethos and expectations, the decision rule, and so on. Norms guide it all, and only some norms are explicit. Thus, the goal of workplace equity is to understand and make visible the norms that people and the organization currently have, and, to be maximally effective and durable, this needs to come from the people through participatory processes of engagement and learning.

Over the past few years, the predominant organizational response to racial and broader social tensions has been a rapid increase in DEI initiatives, committees, and roles. There is cause for concern about the sustainability of these efforts, many of which have already ceased or diminished only a year or two after they began. As Forbes (www.forbes.com/sites/forbescoachescouncil) states,

> While it is clear that the social upheaval events of 2020 have generated a new awakening about the importance of DE&I within the corporate structure, what isn't clear is whether or not this new awakening has opened everyone's eyes to what's needed to make equity less aspirational and more reality.

This speaks to the need for organizational equity efforts to be integrated, positioned as a complex adaptive problem, and not narrowed and reduced by making it a technical problem.

Deloitte's 2021 *The Equity Imperative Report*, states

> Traditionally, organizations have siloed DEI efforts in human resources or have made them discretionary (e.g., philanthropic donations). To drive meaningful change, organizations must view equity as an imperative for its business strategy and all parts of growing the business, incorporating it into every aspect of what they do (e.g., marketing, procurement, finance, technology), at every level of the organization. Workers must hold leaders accountable, and vice versa, rewarding outcomes over activity and valuing impact over intent.

Workplaces all over the world will benefit from better conceptualizations of DEI that build directly from what we have learned from the failures, tensions, and misses of the largely reactive organizational DEI that rolled out during the pandemic.

We see organizational DEI efforts beginning to dry up. Most leaders tell us the efforts were ad hoc and reactive to the racial uprising that reverberated across many parts of the world in the pandemic. The workplace, in aggregate, is feeling the fallout from this scattershot DEI moment; leaders made typically deliberative choices in knee-jerk ways, putting sages on stages whose messages were not relatable or useful to contextual equity issues. Such efforts were often one-offs and siloed, placed squarely in the hands of newly hired DEI officers or committees who were marginalized from mainstream business strategy and organizational functioning, which reflects DEI being treated as a technical problem. DEI cannot be reduced to a technical problem; it is a complex adaptive problem that must be addressed through dynamic and integrative boundary-spanning organizational processes.

Many leaders share with us that the pandemic obscured the ability to do meaningful equity work given physical distance; fewer leaders share that their workplace DEI efforts have been more effective, making long-held biases and experiences of discrimination visible for constructive dialogue and change. From these positive and negative experiences, we offer frames for approaching workplace DEI that can help leaders to build organizational connection and shared understanding. As you cultivate an equity mindset, consider the wisdom gleaned from leaders enacting equity initiatives in their organizations and teams:

- **Learning over certainty:** Focus on inquiry and learning around equity, identity, and bias at all levels of expertise. Question socially constructed notions of expertise to see the kinds of knowledge that exist in many different sources. For example, a CEO recently asked to skip organization-wide equity training because he attended the "same one" last year. He was surprised when we suggested he attend but came to see that his absence would send a loud message to employees that he does not prioritize equity work and/or think he has more to learn on the topic. Equity-focused leaders seek to learn rather than simply perform or impose allyship, knowledge, or expertise.

- **Acknowledge power and privilege:** For some, this may feel counterintuitive and, for others, it may feel offensive, undermining their hard work and struggles. You can interrupt this misunderstanding by stepping into curiosity and accountability. Adaptive leaders sit with their privileges to notice them and to make space for others to do the same; they do this without a savior mentality or virtue signaling. They do not create situations that compare or pit groups against each other, since the goal is to connect, not divide. Do not look away from your privilege even if it feels uncomfortable—even thinking you are entitled to comfort is a privilege many people who work with you simply do not have. Modeling the ability to hold the reality of the privileges you have without falling into traps and tropes of the out-of-it, on-high leader is essential (see Invisible Logic Scans in Chapter One).

- **Question norms:** When introducing equity, diversity, and inclusion, it is vital to understand what has already happened in terms of past programs, bias reporting structures, organizational audits, training, and workshops, and how people with different social identities feel about these efforts. It is equally important to create the conditions for groups and teams to identify and question existing norms together, to consider, for example, who has benefited from the status quo in terms of whose knowledge and communication styles are valued. Reflective questions lead to deepened learning and systemic sense-making: Whose logics are dominant and why? Do current norms of communication dehumanize or marginalize anyone? If so, who and how? How do power and proximity to power shape communication in teams and across the organization? Questioning existing norms for their daily impact on equity and inclusivity from multiple perspectives is vital.

- **Listen actively to people with non-dominant and marginalized identities:** It is a good idea to listen with your lips closed—listen to learn, not to defend yourself or rebut, which misses the point and does not have the effect we hope for. Consider the aspects of bias that apply to you. Do not assume all people with non-dominant identities consider themselves marginalized, do not expect them to necessarily want to talk about it with you, and do not assume they experience the world as you imagine they do (remember the concept of projection from Chapter Two). Considering intersectional identities is a must—people are not just one identity; we are all gendered and raced; we have social class/caste and ethnicity. This helps understand struggles for visibility and tension within marginalized groups.

- **Observe how you react to discomfort:** Raising your threshold for discomfort is vital for impactful professional growth work; it is perhaps the biggest differentiator of adaptive leaders. Do not limit your growth's edge by allowing yourself to slip back into a default comfort zone to avoid the discomfort and tension that identity and equity work can generate. The more authentic and reflective we are, the more we enact and locate workplace equity as the way forward. Notice people who have the ability to sit in discomfort and nurture those relationships.

**Self-reflection** is widely recognized as a vital skill for all leaders. People read the world, and thus DEI, autobiographically. Adaptive leadership is built on a foundation of active and honest self-reflection, introspection into emotions, traits, behaviors, styles, and habits of mind and how they are perceived by others. Self-reflection is a fundamental starting point for the development of emotional intelligence (EQ), which emphasizes awareness and ability to compassionately respond to our emotions and the emotions of others in real time. Self-reflection is the heart of effective and sustainable workplace growth. A growth mindset, Carol Dweck's flagship mindset that frames learning as messy and mistakes and struggles as opportunities for learning and growth, is a useful broad frame for individuals and teams as they enter a reflective path toward organizational equity.

Jennifer Eberhardt (2019) avers that "Bias is not something we exhibit and act on all the time. It is conditional, and the battle begins by understanding the conditions under which it is most likely to come alive". *Self-reflection skills for leaders with dominant identities* include raising self-awareness in relation to recognizing their specific set of privileges, working through reflection and dialogue to excavate their implicit biases, and working to notice racialized and gendered policies, processes, and practices, including daily enactments of microaggressions and other problematic behaviors. Dominant-identity leaders need to be aware that they may unconsciously interpret the behaviors and emotions of people of color and other marginalized identities inaccurately as 'angry' or 'defensive,' which is problematic and which also causes emotional labor. See the societal trope scan in Chapter One for more on this.

*Self-reflection skills for leaders from non-dominant identity groups* include introspection into forms of privilege they have and how these form implicit biases, given how intersectional identities, internalized bias, emotional labor, racial literacy, and the cultivation of a strong sense of self help leaders from non-dominant groups build resilience in the face of bias-laden and discriminatory settings and situations. Understanding the nature of one's own gendered and racialized experiences is an important part of building personal agency. Peer mentoring is a vital strategy; challenge with care is key.

As Abbott (2018) suggests, "People all grow up with the weight of history on us with knowledge hidden in every cell of our bodies." (Abbott, 2018). Every workplace is a collection site for each person's stories, with all their complexity and weight and possibility. Adaptive leaders with an equity mindset are nimble in the face of this profound weight, including what they themselves carry from their own history. Workplace storytelling (discussed in Chapter Two) is a portal to workplace healing and authentic engagement. People must carry equity together.

## Workplace DEI Is a Good Idea, but *Only* When Done Well

DEI, as a workplace equity training framework, has gained new fervor, promising to bring equitable organizational processes and mindsets with it. This work has been happening in organizations for decades, called by many names and often unsuccessful for reasons explored here. For starters, equity work must be designed in ways that are bespoke to an organization and its actual people. Nothing boilerplate does justice to who is in the actual room. Full stop.

The increasing visibility of experiences of workplace bias and discrimination of Black, Asian, Latino, Arab, and LGBTQ+ employees and employees with disabilities has created new accountabilities yet to be fulfilled by most organizations. This is as much about policies as it is about mindsets. Leaders must now create the conditions for employees to cultivate new mindsets and competencies to respond effectively to these new accountabilities through modeling, training, and professional development. As one leader stated, "the risk is that people fall through cracks and stay there." We can story the cracks, all the institutional gaps, through humanizing workplace DEI processes. Leaders can be lead storytellers.

Despite the tremendous promise DEI work and equity-oriented professional development holds, many workplace diversity initiatives are conceptualized and implemented in ways that are untested and decontextualized (as in outsourced boilerplate consultants and programs). These efforts tend to fail or become quickly unsustainable for lack of engagement and positive outcomes, and even at times for fostering negative experiences and outcomes (e.g., frustration, splintering). DEI that does not go well lacks proper conceptualization and scaffolding, typically since leaders do not understand how to judge quality. It does not need to be this way.

Workplace DEI is most effective, relatable, and impactful when it works from an *intersectional approach* to training and professional development. As defined and discussed in Chapter Two, intersectionality means that individual identity consists of multiple intersecting identities, including gender, race, ethnicity, class, religious beliefs, and more. This understanding and framing of identity, in all its lived complexity, creates the conditions for workplace DEI to resonate rather than exclude, to be seen as relevant rather than out of touch and overgeneralized. An intersectional approach to workplace DEI creates multiple entry points to this work in teams and groups. It offers a more strategic and considerably more accurate way to approach diversity, equity, and inclusion, which is both a competency-focused and norms-focused remit.

Most identity complexity and identity-based stress gets lost in current workplace DEI conversations because they quickly become a Black–White binary discussion that excludes and marginalizes a range of people, conflates individuals with systems, and so on. This is not constructive. We regularly hear from Asian, Latino, Arab, Indian, and Native American employees that they are made to feel voiceless in workplace equity conversations and spaces. Clients with disabilities share feeling further 'invisibilized.' The binary construction of racial identity reinforces all sorts of marginalization, misunderstanding, and frustration. DEI should not happen this way. We underscore the importance of affirming intersectional identities and their influence on bias and discrimination as well as opportunity structures, perceptions, experiences, and micro-interactions.

Leaders and organizations can be smarter and braver in their approach to workplace equity; they can proactively address the reality that all oppressions exist and intersect, and that, in fact, organizational and individual well-being depends on it. The application of intersectionality theory (Crenshaw, 1994, 2023) to describe how humans are each and all intersections of different identity markers (e.g., race, gender) is a game changer in relational accountability work in organizations. Everyone has a complex identity—a cultural story, a racialized identity (whether taught to think this way or not), a gendered and classed/casted story.

Impactful workplace DEI should not only engage *part* of people's identities and surely should not pit groups and their histories against each other for recognition of oppression. It must affirm everyone's history, view all oppressions as both interconnected and distinct, and compassionately explore how people live in their layered identities within systems of privilege and discrimination, with a focus on the workplace. It is about humanizing everyone because, in truth, everyone is complex and suffering on some level—this is the human condition. It is about understanding that some people and groups suffer more, in a diffusion effect caused by discriminatory systems, in ways that others do not (again, both/ and thinking means all this can be true simultaneously). Jennifer Eberhardt (2019) reminds us that "We choose what to pay attention to based on the ideas that we already have in our heads".

A useful frame for understanding this workplace DEI phenomenon is that many current enactments of workplace DEI operate from scarcity logics (there are only so many resources, suffering, and acclaim to go around) and deficit perspectives (specific people and groups are viewed as problematic and deficient) about diversity and equity. A deficit perspective relates to the tendency to see people from specific cultural, racial, or gender groups as less than oneself, lacking abilities and strengths because of their social identity background. Deficit orientations focus on perceived weaknesses of individuals and groups, such that the individuals or groups become viewed as 'the problem.'

Together, scarcity logics and deficit orientations amplify tensions, at times even creating new ones. Adaptive leaders work from an abundance logic about the world and resource orientation toward people, meaning they are appreciative, humanizing, and equitable; they affirm individual and group courage and appreciate intergroup and intragroup diversity rather than essentializing identity groups based on racial, cultural, or gender characteristics. Adaptive leaders and workplaces offer employees humanization through constructively critical knowledge creation. Shirley Abbott's (2018) insight that "We all grow up with the weight of history on us. Our ancestors dwell in the attics of our brains as they do in the spiraling chains of knowledge hidden in every cell of our bodies" is evergreen.

## Name and Reframe Bias to Address It

Bias is an integral part of the human condition. Prejudice and misunderstanding are endemic to being human. People become grounded in certain views and opinions—prejudgments, biases, or prejudices—by virtue of their experiences in the world. These perspectives contribute to their understandings and misunderstandings of other people's experiences and perspectives. Accordingly, biases and prejudices are ideally not viewed as markers of social ignorance or flawed character. Rather, they are best reframed as openings for increased understanding and more honest and aware communication. Whether you think of them as implicit or unconscious biases, they are imprinted on us, yet unconscious.

Theresa McHenry of Marketing and Consumer Business at Microsoft asserts, "The point isn't to get people to accept that they have biases, but to get them to see [for themselves] that those biases have negative consequences for others" (McHenry, 2020). Implicit biases must be continuously identified and revised through explicit reflection processes of uncovering and confrontation using dialogue and self-reflection. People's thoughts, communications, interactions, and interpretations cannot be abstracted from the constraints and possibilities of the larger societal forces in which they are embedded. In this sense, uncovering is intended to make explicit the societal forces that shape interpretations which influence action.

From this perspective, it is problematic to choose not to explore our own biases and prejudices and the contexts that shape them. The lack of such exploration impedes serious (and often uncomfortable) consideration of the (mis) understandings that result from our biased interpretations. Without careful consideration of our preconceived notions about other people, we work from an overly constricted worldview and, consequently, a limited understanding of the various influences on the work we do and the relationships we form. Given the vicissitudes of experience that influence interpretation, there is infinite room for misunderstanding others and for being misunderstood (Nakkula & Ravitch, 1998).

Misunderstanding and miscommunication occur even within the closest relationships and between people from similar ethnic or cultural backgrounds. Given how society is structured, these phenomena become more prevalent in cross-cultural, cross-generational, cross-race, and cross-class/cross-caste work. Within professional contexts, differences in interpretive authority, privilege, and institutional power exacerbate possibilities for acting from misunderstanding. Because there are infinite possibilities for misunderstanding and misappropriating other people's meanings, even with the best intentions, people must expect this and meet it with curious intention (Nakkula & Ravitch, 1998).

Actualizing hope for growth and change relies on the commitment to self-reflection, reflecting on our biases and prejudices, background, worldview, and perspectives on others. It also requires ongoing analysis of how these issues play out in workplace communication. We can never (and, we would argue, should not want to) secure ourselves with the belief that perspective is neutral, objective, or unencumbered by experiences with and notions about individuals and groups. Instead, we must recognize that our work always holds the possibility of being influenced by counterproductive prejudices, some of which lie outside our awareness. By increasing self-reflection as a continual effort to contextualize ourselves and others within the multiple contexts of life—constructions of race, class, ethnicity, gender, politics, and culture, and relational and individual particulars—there is opportunity for self-awareness and perspective-taking abilities to take root and blossom.

Interpretation reaches into our psychological worlds, shaping what we value, our styles of communication, our relationships, and how society at large functions. Acts of interpretation are pervasive and subtle, and people often take our own values and perspectives for granted as 'the way things are' or 'the right perspective' when they are actually our own socialized belief systems that are socially and contextually constructed. Working with intention to uncover underlying assumptions that inform our interpretations is a vital foundation for learning agility. Transformation does not imply trying to 'do away' with our biases; rather, it means actively modifying them in the face of new and contradictory awareness. Such transformation of our perspectives (even those we cherish) leads to maximizing our positive impact. As Nakkula and Ravitch (1998) state,

> Differences of opinion, worldview, cultural background, and life experience all serve as fuel for the dialogical process. To recognize and engage with difference requires the willingness to acknowledge misunderstanding and to be misunderstood. ... Genuine empathy cannot be achieved without an authentic willingness to misunderstand, to strive to connect only to miss the point, and as such to feel disengaged. All too frequently, false connections are maintained to salve the discomfort of disconnection. A productive synthesis of differences requires a grappling with discomfort, a clear recognition of disjunctions. Willingness to reach toward understanding amid such discomforting misconnections is ... a healthy prognosis for mutual growth.

Understanding the need to allow oneself to become vulnerable in relationships is at the heart of the work of collaboration building; everyone needs a receptive sensibility, people must not only see and acknowledge differences, but see them as valuable and generative "funds of knowledge" (González et al., 2005). It speaks to the need to allow ourselves to become more openly vulnerable, inwardly reflexive, and consciously collaborative to raise our thresholds for the discomfort that engaging and transforming our work requires.

## Learning Frames and Activations for an Equity Mindset

### Tool 1: Equity 2.0: Workplaces as Brave Spaces

When discussing issues that some people find difficult or in which they have firmly held beliefs, a common solution is to create 'safe spaces' for conversation. The term safe space connotes a place in which everyone feels comfortable to speak their mind and share their experiences, ideas, concerns, and so on. However, the concept of safe spaces can be a setup for non-dominant identity groups because 'safe' means different things to different people, based on how they have been socialized. What feels safe to one person could feel hostile, inauthentic, or negligent to another. In contrast to safe spaces, *brave spaces* require group bravery so that people can raise authentic questions and issues that reflect their lived experiences. They enable dialogue to go a layer deeper than what is typically discussed in the workplace.

The discussion of the contrast between safe spaces and brave spaces within teams and organizations is powerful. How people's interpersonal approaches are differentially valued, engaged with, and respected reflects integrated workplace biases. For example, teams with unexamined issues of implicit bias often play out and weaponize societal tropes: the well-meaning White woman who tries to be racially aware but says offensive things and is overly emotional about her own pain and guilt at society's inequity; the Black woman who is (mis)interpreted as an angry Black woman before she ever even speaks; the White man who tries to eschew his race and gender privilege by talking about his family's meritocracy story.

There are also countless people who do not fall into these essentialized identity category buckets. However, it is important that there are cultural identity tropes that everyone needs to be thoughtful about in order to read the room accurately and adjust themselves. Processes that attend to this enable people to level up their relational skills, which rely on emotional and cultural intelligence. Structured exercises to get people to look underneath the ingrained biases that people and the organization hold are vital. This must happen in ways that humanize and connect people as equal human beings. As elder Lilla Watson (1994) states, "If you have come here to help me, you are wasting your time, but if you have come here because your liberation is bound up with mine, then let us work together" (Watson, 1994). This is the vision and the remit of organizational equity and humanization.

## Building Equity through Cultivating Brave Spaces

The concept of safe versus brave spaces comes from social justice work in higher education settings, from an observation that safe spaces reinforce current power dynamics and limit the possibility of disrupting inequity (Arao & Clemens, 2013). Brave spaces, where discomfort is shared and expected as a part of group authenticity, illuminate to disrupt the reality that systems are doing what they were designed to do: perpetuate current power structures and dynamics. Brave spaces are environments that encourage equal and authentic participation for everyone. Bravery is necessary, instead of safety, because creating new norms necessarily involves risk and the pain of giving up privileges in favor of more equitable ways of doing things. It means people must do the work to see, and name, and work on, their implicit biases. It also means that groups work to uncover sedimented workplace and team norms that undermine equity.

Brave spaces necessitate intentional communication and process norms that create the conditions for more authentic, equitable dialogue and humanizing engagement in groups, teams, and organizations. Brave spaces foreground the importance of people being brave and safe enough to enter spaces where they can be their authentic selves and share personal lived experiences of and beyond the workplace. Brave spaces lay the foundation for team and organizational communicative processes to be proactive and compassionate rather than reactive and divisive. They require, as they evince, honesty, reflection, and boundary setting.

Brave spaces encourage equitable dialogue, engagement with difference, and accountability in sharing experiences to come to new understandings— something that is often difficult and uncomfortable in work life. Brave spaces operationalize appreciative inquiry to support compassionate perspective-taking; they disrupt knowledge siloes and help to locate structural equity problems. Many workplace DEI initiatives fail *before they roll out* because they are ill conceived in terms of how to facilitate equitable group dialogue. Their failure reinforces the belief that workplace diversity work is a bad idea. Brave spaces offer an alternative to this negative cycle.

Brave spaces support meaningful workplace DEI by priming people to take personal responsibility and relational accountability for the implications of their identity-based stress, imposed assumptions, disenfranchising habits, and deficit-based behaviors. An equity mindset helps leaders and teams name problematic communication norms and set intentional norms that drive equity. This happens when groups actively reflect together on how individuals make meaning and show up in the group, along with what they feel, know, see, and need in teams. Creating brave space norms and critiquing the status quo as drivers of more equitable communication surface insights that might otherwise be neglected or misunderstood. When done effectively, brave space norming processes are humanizing, connecting, and uplifting for everyone, evincing professional transformation.

Brave space processes help leaders identify problematic communication norms that reduce workplace creativity and authenticity and limit disruptive innovation. Once a leader decides to shift to an equity-focused organizational model, re-norming group communication becomes an opportunity to dislodge old habits and routines that no longer serve the organization well. This requires observation, reflection, issue identification, and examination of existing norms. As part of norming, groups identify communication patterns including bias, tension, invisibility, emotional labor, and microaggressions together. This helps people connect the concept of brave spaces to their own experience, to other people's experiences, and to their own behavior without promoting defensiveness, which supports recalibration of unexamined team processes.

Brave spaces must be designed in ways that are bespoke to each organization, team, and group. They do share these common guidelines that can be customized:

- **Agree to disagree:** This means shared acceptance of diverse opinions and perspectives as a foundational tenet of group life and communication.
- **Own impact over intention:** This requires that each person commit to acknowledging when they affect someone's well-being regardless of intent.
- **Challenge by choice:** This means that each person has the option to step in and out of challenging conversations to take care of themselves.
- **Respect:** This means all members agree to acknowledge and show respect for everyone's humanity.
- **No attacks:** This is a shared agreement that it is unacceptable to inflict harm through personal attacks, slights, or sharing confidential information.

Luminary and civil rights activist Audre Lorde (1984) offers, "It is not our differences that divide us. It is our inability to recognize, accept, and celebrate those differences" (Lorde, 1984). For people with various kinds of identity-based privilege, it is useful to remember that brave space learning and growth may require you to:

1. Notice, evaluate, and give up former habits for new ways of doing things.
2. Engage in conversation even when fearing you will get it wrong. Accept feedback about an insensitivity, uninformed perspective, implicit bias, or microaggression.
3. Slow down your nervous system, which has been primed to panic when we are called out on our biases. Move into a growth mindset and commit to active learning. Remember that you, like all humans, are always on the way.
4. Work to understand **emotional labor**—the need employees feel to protect the feelings of those from dominant groups with power, which includes enduring microaggressions and being inauthentic to fit a universalized professional ideal. Non-dominant identity groups are judged by dominant group standards, creating the need for inauthenticity, an invisible tax of emotional labor caused by pressure to conform to White standards of behavior and communication. The concept of emotional labor illuminates how workplaces are designed to benefit those with the most power, including proximal power (see emotional labor scans in Chapter One).
5. Work to understand **intent versus impact**. *Intent* is your goal when you decide to act—your intention. It reflects the impact *you want to create* with your actions. *Impact* is the result of those actions. The results are not necessarily what you intended. Impact reflects the reality of your actions. Impact in the workplace matters because it determines the reality of everyone who

works there. Clear communication is only possible when intent and impact are both considered. When intent and impact are elucidated, teams can collaborate to find generative solutions. It is vital to step into your accountability rather than hide in your intent when called out on your biases; this is how adaptive leaders traverse tensions effectively and teach others to do the same.

6. Learn about and enact **bystander intervention**, which is recognizing a potentially harmful interaction and choosing to respond to positively influence the outcome. Steps include: (1.) *Notice the event.* Pay attention. (2.) *Interpret it as a possible problem.* Err on the side of caution and investigate. (3.) *Assume personal responsibility.* Assume that you need to do something, that no one else will. (4.) *Know how to help.* Help can be direct or indirect. (5.) *Implement the help.* Speak up. Relatedly, an **ally** acts against oppression out of a belief that eliminating oppression will benefit members of targeted groups and advantaged groups. An **accomplice** assists others in creating inclusion, equity, and safety for all, often at the risk of their own social or professional standing.

7. For White people specifically, just as people of color do not have the luxury of expecting a right to comfort in groups, neither should you. Do your homework on this topic to realize how you show up, even though you may be unaware you are being viewed in these ways because it is off your radar and out of your purview. The expectation of the right to comfort is an articulation of entitlement.

For those with non-dominant identities, it is useful to remember that brave space learning and growth may mean that you:

1. Recognize that being in these kinds of group discussions may make you feel vulnerable, exposed, frustrated, and/or angry. The only choice is to be safe.
2. Recognize the surprise and weight people feel when their blind spots and the work they must do are illuminated, often for the first time in front of their colleagues.
3. Elevate marginalized voices; your and their knowing is vital and should be foregrounded.
4. Remember that these conversations tend to happen within a White gaze; make sure not to feed into Black–White identity binaries or deficit orientations about other non-dominant group members.
5. Stay present in your body using CLCBE (calculate, locate, communicate, breathe, and exhale) as an identity-based stress navigation and mindfulness tool.

Many people have privileged *and* minoritized identities; they should not be invisible. Remember, safety is subjective and mediated by power. People's interpretations of communication are mediated by social identity, power, and hierarchy. The term *safe space* suggests a place where everyone feels comfortable speaking freely and sharing their experiences, feelings, and concerns authentically. However, the concept of safe spaces can be a setup for people with less proximal power because power weights whose version of safety wins. Workplaces are collection sites for inequitable communication norms, unappreciative communication, and implicit biases until leaders decide this is no longer appropriate or acceptable.

## Tool 2: Norms Scan for a Re-norming Plan

As society becomes increasingly polarized, people must work to develop and improve their skills to manage interpersonal and organizational conflict and constructively address workplace bias. Creating authentic communication norms engages groups in reflective and constructive dialogue. For this reason, we offer a set of ideas for creating guidelines for authentic dialogue.

### Framing: Improving Communication Norms in Groups Requires Practice

### Consideration of Brave Space Questions

1. Think about the spaces you inhabit. Who are those spaces safe for? Who are they not safe for? How do you know?
2. If you come from a place of privilege, how often do you think about the lack of authenticity your colleagues with marginalized identities may feel around you and others?
3. Where do you feel authentic, inauthentic, and brave?
4. What does lack of psychological safety feel like for you? Where do you feel it in your body? How do you react, think, do?
5. What is your commitment to authenticity and self-reflection?

As with all practices in this book, customization, and adaptation to make norms relevant to context are generative. Group norms are influenced by many factors, including membership, familiarity, styles of engagement, leader values, and time.

### Expectation Setting

For those with privileged identities, it can help to remember that brave space learning and growth may mean that you:

1. Give up former habits for new ways of doing things.
2. Engage in conversation even when fearing you will get it wrong.

3.  Accept feedback about an insensitivity, uninformed perspective, implicit biases, or microaggressions.
4.  Slow down your nervous system, which has been primed to panic when called out on your biases. Move into a growth mindset and actively learn. Remember that people are always on the way.
5.  For White people, explore the reality that, just as people of color do not have the luxury of expecting a right to comfort in groups, neither do you. Do your homework on this to realize how you are showing up— you are likely unaware of ways you are viewed because it is out of your purview. The expectation of the right to comfort is an articulation of entitlement.

For those with non-dominant identities, it can help to remember that brave space learning and growth may mean that you:

1.  Recognize that being in these discussions may make you feel vulnerable, exposed, frustrated, and/or angry. The only choice is to be safe.
2.  Recognize the weight people feel when their blind spots and the work they must do are illuminated, often for the first time in public.
3.  Elevate your and other marginalized voices; your/their knowing is vital and should be foregrounded.
4.  Remember that these conversations tend to happen within a White gaze; make sure not to feed into Black–White binaries or deficit orientations about marginalized identity groups.
5.  Stay present in your body using CLCBE as an identity-based stress navigation and mindfulness tool.

## Norms Scan

1.  Meet as an inquiry group, in teams, or as a whole group.
    Reflect on and brainstorm existing communication norms—what are current expectations of communication? How are these enforced? What, if anything, do they limit?
2.  List tacit norms and discuss them across perspectives and roles.
3.  Reimagine communication norms to be more useful and inclusive.
4.  Decide on a call-in, rather than call-out, approach to relational and group accountability. The concept of a cancel and call-out culture is defined by swift public admonishment upon a perceived transgression. *Calling people in* means constructively addressing oppressive behaviors and structures from within relationships to drive compassionate accountability.
5.  Discuss opportunities for structured collaboration through inquiry groups as professional development around workplace equity.

## *Norm-Setting*

1. Create a starter list of norms, perhaps between five and eight, by going around the room for ideas, ensuring that everyone shares at least one idea.
2. As a group, priority rank these norms thoughtfully. Discuss each one, asking for clarification on their ranking.
3. Decide how norms will be learned and reinforced (e.g., in upcoming meetings, on teams).
4. After a selected period (1–2 weeks), hold a norms debrief and produce a progress report.
5. Refine norms; add norms or take away ones that do not fit or seem extraneous. Finalize the list together through dialogue.

## *Brave Space Listening and Discovery Sessions*

Brave space listening and discovery sessions are active listening and perspective-taking sessions. Be thoughtful about groupings along the lines of power and confidentiality. Consider communities of practice and/or affinity groups as possible structures that support these processes. Debrief sessions are useful to plan forward with transparency.

1. **Introduce the concept of brave spaces:** Ask people why they think you chose this term instead of *safe space*. Discuss why you chose it and map it onto organizational and personal values to foreground.
2. **Set the stage for success:** Engaging authentically before getting to communication norms can sometimes require setting a group intention; here is an example:
   At [Company], we hold ourselves accountable and take responsibility for creating respectful dialogue. We encourage risk-taking and support challenge with care on important issues to promote reciprocal learning. We work to authentically discuss differing perspectives through active listening. We recognize that everyone holds socialized points of view and give grace as we learn new ones.
3. **Discuss** how you can create and protect this brave space together.
4. **Model openness** to ideas, involve everyone, and affirm input, engaging people if they struggle with the concept of brave spaces.
5. **Discuss** what authenticity and bravery means for an organization/team/individual.
6. **Set norms** together and create a summary available to everyone.
7. **Groups develop and review norms:** Consider how norms mediate authentic and productive dialogue. People reflect on how they want to feel at work.
8. **Refine, adjust, discuss:** The process generates emergent relational learning, not something to get through quickly.

9. **Reinforce the value** of bravery and authenticity in subsequent meetings. Brave spaces are a generative topic for inquiry groups. Self-selected affinity groups are a structure that works in many workplace settings.

## Tool 3: Racial Literacy: Identify and Navigate Identity-Based Stress

There is no panacea for addressing identity-based stress that emerges during conversations about equity, race, even vaccines and masks in the current moment in the United States. A first step to building an equity mindset is to create an individualized equity action plan. The first item on that action plan is cultivating identity-based stress navigation tools and racial literacy and mindfulness skills to navigate, learn, and thrive in an intensely polarizing time (and beyond). To be clear, racial literacy now takes up intersectional identities and is inclusive to everyone since everyone has a racial identity.

Navigating identity-based stress is a professional skill everyone needs to thrive in the workplace. Equity-focused leaders understand there are always varying levels of self-awareness and tolerance for disagreement and tension; they create the conditions for everyone in the organization to practice mindful communication so that interactions and collaboration can happen through an empowerment framework. A leader's racial literacy skills enable them to cultivate (1.) a more authentically engaged workplace ethos; (2.) increased capacity to cultivate effective systems, norms, and processes; (3.) humanization, connection, care, and belonging; and (4.) an environment that values the prevention and de-escalation of disagreements and promotes authentic engagement through constructive confrontation and adaptive learning.

### CLCBE Identity-Based Stress Management Tool

Dr. Howard Stevenson's (2014) CLCBE racial stress and mindfulness and management model helps people learn how to manage their identity-based stress in the workplace. In his racial literacy training, Dr. Stevenson shares the West African proverb, "The lion's story will never be known as long as the hunter is the one to tell it," to frame the need for organizational courage to hear stories through the veil of power.

**CLCBE** can be taught and practiced in 45–60 minutes and then used as a tool for managing and learning from stressful encounters based on identity. CLCBE was popularized by Dr. Stevenson's TED Talks on racial literacy and navigating identity-based stress; it is an efficient and impactful professional development and life skills training program. This approach helps us manage our amygdala (flight or fight response) during tense and upsetting interactions, can be learned quickly, and, with practice, becomes a daily practice that is instinctual in moments of stress.

**CLCBE** stands for calculate, locate, communicate, breathe, and exhale:

1. **Calculate it:** On a scale of 1–10, how stressful was the racially stressful encounter? Did it shift, spike over the arc of the event?
2. **Locate it:** Find in your body where you feel the stress; try to be as detailed as possible to locate how and where you feel the stress in your body.
3. **Communicate it:** Name the feelings and sensations you feel as you feel them: *I'm feeling stressed at the level of 9, I feel it as pressure in my chest, and I'm sweating profusely.*
4. **Breathe and exhale:** Breathe in 5–5–5—that is, breathe in for 5 seconds, hold for 5 seconds, exhale for 5 seconds.

**CLCBE** is a game-changer for leaders, teams, and organizations. It is a proven stress-reduction model that teaches entire organizations how to productively *process and resolve identity-based stress* at a time when it is brewing and spilling over into workplaces in a range of ways, both obvious and insidious. Develop intentions and routines around CLCBE that foster new kinds of connection, meaningful engagement, and emotional benevolence rather than distrust, depersonalization, and emotional scarcity. The spirit of this is healing and growth.

## Racial Literacy

New accountability for workplace equity is a long time coming. Leaders are accountable in new ways for organizational culture, which includes building skills and an ecosystem for addressing microaggressions, enactments of bias, and dominating workplace behaviors. Being racially literate means creating the conditions in which people can cultivate racial literacy and identity-based stress navigation skills.

A racially literate leader understands that there are varying levels of racial literacy, self-awareness, and thresholds for tension within teams and groups. Building racial literacy skills empowers individuals and contributes to a more authentically and positively engaged organization. Racial literacy helps teams to cultivate equitable practices that help to prevent or de-escalate tensions and disagreements. This elevates relational accountability.

If racial literacy were to be put into poetry, Nayyirah Waheed's (2013) words would reflect its essence: "Some people when they hear your story contract. others upon hearing expand. And this is how you know" (2013). Racial literacy enables people to expand their compassion and self-awareness born in a work culture that values both. Racial literacy, according to its creator, Dr. Howard Stevenson, is the ability to read, recast, and resolve stress *during* racially stressful encounters:

- **Read** = decode racial subtexts, sub-codes, and scripts.
- **Recast** = reduce stress in stressful encounters using racial mindfulness.
- **Resolve** = negotiate racially stressful encounters to a healthy conclusion.

Racial literacy involves enacting tools and coping strategies in racially stressful moments (remember that 100% of people have racial stress, whether they are consciously processing it or not). It is a vital skill in which to build fluency, because, when left unaddressed, identity-based conflicts hurt our physical and mental health, well-being, and cognitive functioning. Being racially literate and leading a racially literate organization means creating the conditions in which you and the people in your organization can cultivate racial literacy and identity-based stress navigation skills through skills-focused professional development.

During these learning moments, it is useful to remind people that: (1.) racial stress is distinct from general stress and requires specific skills; (2.) it is vital to approach racial literacy as a practice of racial competence, not as an issue of flawed character; (3.) organizations and teams are generally socialization hubs of avoidant and dysfunctional racial coping; and (4.) resolving racial stress in everyday life leads to better learning and life experiences and health outcomes (Stevenson, 2014).

Understanding where you are on the continuum of racial literacy happens through continued practice of "courageous noticing and admitting" to self (Edwards, 2016)—about your own patterns of identity-based tension, conflict, and struggle. Dr. Howard Stevenson's work on racial literacy and navigating identity-related stress situates racial mindfulness as a central node of leadership.

Developing your racial literacy and identity-related stress navigation skills happens through engaging in the CLCBE practices of self-reflection and dialogic engagement, with a focus on a recent racially stressful encounter: *What did I notice about myself in the moment? How stressed did I feel and where/how did it affect my body? What did I hold back during the racially stressful encounter out of fear? If I had a do-over, what would I say or do differently to read, recast, and resolve the encounter? Do I have healthy racial comeback lines? What could those sound like? Can I practice them with a trusted person? Am I prepared for the next face-to-face racial encounter, and how can I be?* Building the confidence and skills for future encounters is part of building racial mindfulness as individuals and in groups (Stevenson, 2014).

## Tool 4: Backstage-Processing Relationships

Based on her research on how people with dominant-group identities best learn to work effectively in cross-identity work relationships, Marcy Crary (2017), professor of management at Bentley University, offers backstage-processing relationships.

**Backstage-processing relationships** support intentional work on bias and identity-based stress navigation skills. Backstage-processing thought partners are typically not directly involved in the interactions or situations in question, nor are they necessarily part of the context in which the interactions took place. These dialogic engagement partners help us question how we interpret complicated interpersonal dynamics, which surfaces our implicit biases, our patterns of conflict and misunderstanding, and our possible role in creating problems and harm.

Through working on our areas of necessary growth and defensiveness off in the distance, where no one can see, we enable our employees and colleagues to get a more practiced version of us, one that is more thoughtful and less apt to fall into default modes of behavior that do harm.

Crary suggests that the ability to construct mutual understanding and positive interactions presents a challenge when working across social identities, which requires navigating complex identity intersections at work. Dialogue and navigation in cross-race interactions can be complex, requiring awareness of broader structural issues related to identity, power, hierarchy, and status. Equitable engagement is not one size fits all; it is contextual. Thus, it is vital to surround ourselves with people who are more advanced in their racial and cultural awareness and can help us take a perspective on ourselves more fully since they are farther ahead in this work than we are. Leaders, like their employees, need help in reflecting on confusing cross-race work interactions; this requires active support to consider alternative interpretations of, and responses to, the situation.

High-quality peer mentoring relationships can be brave spaces that enable people to stretch their adaptive capacity to live in the learning and growth zones when it comes to anti-racism. Building on Crary's suggestions, additional support modalities for transformative dialogue and leader self-reflection, learning, and growth include:

## *Relational Resources*

1. Cross-identity dialogic engagement
2. Affinity and identity-based groups
3. Peer-mentoring activities and groups
4. Backstage-processing groups
5. Role models and intergenerational mentoring

## *Individual Resources*

1. Motivation to care about equity and interpersonal dynamics
2. Identification and active addressing of own biases, strengths, and weaknesses
3. Accumulation of knowledge of typical identity-based challenges
4. Self-guidelines for adaptive learning in this space
5. Education of self and others rather than internalization of external biases

# Equity Mindset Activations

## *Try Now*

1. Remember: Logical thinking and emotional distress are in an inverse relationship. Triggers activate the brain's adrenal system, which governs emotion

(as in adrenalin). This, in turn, eclipses the brain's logical functioning system (limbic system). Develop your inner stress management skills through building a space between stimulus and response and cultivating identity-based stress management skills. Breathe slowly and deeply, which shifts brain activity when we are anxious. Take breaks for stretching and breathing.

2.  Consider beginning meetings with stress-reduction activities such as breathing exercises, given pervasively high stress levels. Provide engaging learning structures that promote inner calm amid change.
3.  Identify an equity "accountabilibuddy" for ongoing dialogue and learning.
4.  Consider structuring your executive team as an inquiry group to explore communication norms and identity-based dynamics; build this into meetings.

## Build a Weekly Practice

1.  Call on trusted people to hold you accountable for how you react to discomfort and stress. Develop a process for racial literacy development equity call-in; challenge with care.
2.  Pick someone to engage in shared self-reflection, dialogic engagement, and peer mentoring around communication styles and emergent ideas and issues.
3.  Build an inquiry group model for discussing equity and developing racial literacy. Inquiry groups support developing identity-based stress navigation skills and foster the conditions for effectively identifying, naming, and pushing against real-time inequities on teams and in the organization as a whole.
4.  Develop, disseminate, and analyze with your team, using pulse surveys, brief open-ended questionnaires, flash interviews, listening sessions, and multimodal data elicitation. Set up an internal task force and/or external advisory group.

## Try Monthly

1.  Recalibrate the structure, content, or duration of meetings and professional development sessions.
2.  Re-envision communication and process norms by naming harmful dynamics. Discuss reciprocity of efforts to set norms.
3.  Plan *listening and discovery sessions* with different organizational groups, formal and informal. Engage in active listening and structured perspective-taking processes. Be thoughtful about groupings with respect to hierarchy and confidentiality.
4.  Find a thought partner (and inquiry group) to debrief these sessions and plan forward in ways that affirm people's experiences and respond to their concerns.

# CONCLUSION

## Leader as 'the Space between No Longer and Not Yet'

You are a pioneer, charting new territory on unknown terrain, without clear coordinates or tracks to follow. Speaking on current workplace precarity, author and corporate coach Nancy Levin (2015) invites leaders to "Honor the space between no longer and not yet" as a way to integrate all that has happened and everything they and their organizations have experienced with what they now want to create and achieve. This liminal space is where leader resilience, possibility, and opportunity converge and amplify each other. We add that this moment requires leaders not just to honor but to *build* the space between no longer and not yet to move their teams and organizations forward.

As a practice framework, Flux 5 helps you cultivate mindsets and practices to grow yourself, your executive team, and your organization, to build the space of adaptive change. How you prioritize and use these mindsets and practices is contextual and temporal; it will change as your organization's needs, issues, and opportunities shift and emerge. As you practice—yourself, with your team, and in the wider organization—you will notice increased freedom in choosing what is necessary for specific kinds of changes, crises, and opportunities. Mindset work helps leaders, teams, and organizations make meaningful sense of it all in real time, surfacing sedimented logics that inhibit learning, growth, and innovation and fostering adaptive change. Mindsets drive behavior and action, and action drives outcomes in a cyclical fashion.

Adaptive leaders *build and serve as* the space between no longer and not yet—a bridge to a calm now and hopeful future in times of insecurity, confusion, and change. *Being the space between no longer and not yet* is what we mean by *leaders as portals*—leading their people into new workplace mindsets and realities that disrupt stale status quo workplace norms, mindsets, policies, and processes.

DOI: 10.4324/b23253-7

*Being* the space between no longer and not yet requires adaptive risk-taking to drive informed workplace equity, inquiry, humanization, innovation, and systems sustainability.

The concept of a hybrid space is referred to as "third spaces" by critical theorist Homi Bhabha (2004) and social psychologist Lev Vygotsky (1978), who argue that Industrial Age rationality, with its dehumanizing and reductive logics, policies, and systems, created a paradigm of work that undermines humanization, purpose, and trust (what Roy, 2020, refers to as "the doomsday machine we have built for ourselves").

As an antidote, and possibility framework, Bhabha and Vygotsky argue from their respective fields for the intentional creation of third spaces—creative thought partnership spaces that exist separately from and parallel to formal spaces—in which people can step back, take perspective, engage in generative dialogue, and reflect. Third spaces are creative in-between spaces from which support and growth emerge, spaces of exploration, inquiry, authenticity, and humanization. When designed and implemented well, *workplace DEI can be a third space* that helps groups accomplish these goals and build individual, team, and organizational adaptability.

Speaking on the losses generated by Industrial Age rationality, Nobel Prize-winning economist Amartya Sen (2004) implores humanity to reclaim who we can be as he writes, "It is important to reclaim for humanity the ground that has been taken from it by various arbitrarily narrow formulations of the demands of rationality." Such various and narrow formulations include, for example, hyper compliance-driven HR offices and policies that institutionalize harm of people in lower-level positions to protect those higher up as an artifact of dehumanization, or when an organization treats employees as worthless through multiple acts that constitute 'demoralization by a thousand paper cuts.' Rationality created the conditions for a lack of workplace compassion and humanization that persists in many workplaces to this day. The time to reclaim this ground for humanity is now, and leaders do this by challenging **current** *narrow formulations of the demands of rationality* through identifying them in workplace systems, processes, and mindsets. Widening cracks in the foundation of rationality have let light in, illuminating a path to more equitable and humanizing organizations.

Creative third spaces can serve teams and organizations well in this time of dramatic polarities and an epidemic of overly rigid, black-and-white, all-or-nothing thinking; they offer a self-made and reinforcing learning ecosystem cultivated through processes that enable people to be curious about, and calmly reckon with, the far corners of our psyches. We do this by shining soft light on our thought patterns to illuminate rather than shame ourselves. This reflexive stance makes *self-care* possible, especially for those of us ready to 'do our work' as we simultaneously stop doing other people's work, and for others of us ready to shed the unnecessary *emotional labor* that shapes our daily realities and to turn to ourselves—as the experts and learners of ourselves—in ways that enable us to build self-knowledge, accountability, and grounded appreciation of self.

As discussed in Chapter One on an inquiry mindset, when we allow curiosity in, we can see ourselves, our choices, and our behaviors in their contextual frames—historical, current, imagined. To understand what is happening within interpersonal situations warrants self-reflection and situational reflection to discover our role and discern the learning we still need to do. When we soothe our anxious or defensive impulses, we open ourselves up to learning what we need to unlearn—behaviors that once served us well that have become maladaptive (as the theory goes, we develop habits that may have served us well early in our lives but do not translate into positive adult mindsets/behaviors and therefore become harmful rather than protective). When we quiet our nervous system, we can locate the true source of our stress and learn how to manage it quite well.

The parable is clear: Leaders must both create and serve as third spaces in which employees can learn in transformational ways together, come to understand and rely on each other, and deepen authenticity and relational trust. *Institutional and interpersonal holding*, discussed in Chapter Two, helps leaders enact third spaces that make work more equitable, humanizing, and dynamic. Leaders do this through activating dynamic reflection within their spheres of influence and by modeling presence, curiosity, compassion, and relational commitment and care.

The Flux 5 framework is customizable to context and real-time situations, team processes, goals, and organizational strategies. In our work with leaders and teams, we see engaging these mindsets as its own reward, building momentum as the learning process generates new energy, optimism, connection, and resilience that have a significant impact on collective well-being. The Conclusion offers five conceptual frames to support learning integration as you bring adaptive change forward into your leadership, teams, and organization.

## Leaders Are Portals

As Pak and Ravitch wrote to leaders in 2021, "Everyone is hurting and the whole world is in pain. Leaders must proceed thus." These are profound truths that leaders must reckon with as, at time of writing, we collectively enter the third year of a global pandemic. With all that is happening in the world and in people's lives, people yearn for a place to name, understand, and process their stress and trauma—for their experiences to be heard and validated, to feel affirmed and connected, and to gain a sense of control over their lives. With so much time spent working (the current average is 48 hours per week at work in the United States), changing values around what work means (or does not mean or should mean), and the new kinds of purpose people newly seek to derive from their professional lives, leaders must learn to address the changing meaning of work.

In pandemic workplace research, 72% of employees express the need for their leaders to be more responsive to their needs to make work reasonable and sustainable. Leaders need to know how to respond to a new range of intense emerging needs, including post-pandemic recalibration impacts on people's finances, family responsibilities, and necessary professional scaffolds and supports. Leaders need to newly learn how to centralize employee well-being, build new kinds of relational trust, teach people to view adaptive change as a skill and stance, and work collaboratively to shake siloed knowledge and communication norms to elicit diverse wisdom and generate authentic engagement and optimal performance.

Employees need active support to build inner resources for calm in conflict, crisis, and change. Attention to this aspect of workplace well-being is a necessary foundation for learning, collaboration, and professional development in a social moment rife with intense division. This social and political moment around the world invokes a new leadership remit in which *the relational must supersede the transactional.* This requires leaders to enact, and model, active self-reflection, equity awareness and accountability, empathy and active listening, transparency, and trust. These build shared purpose and relational trust, the foundation for strengths-based professional development.

To be a portal to others' growth, you must want to grow yourself. Practicing self-care has never been more urgent or elusive for leaders than in this socially, politically, economically, environmentally, and spiritually intense time. Calls for self-care are loud in public discourse and the media sales cycle frenzy, yet few leaders take the time to consider what their own needs are for wellness, self-care, or even personal and professional growth.

It can be difficult to shift to a focus on personal wellness and self-care when grind culture has been lifted as a badge of honor and a signal of virtue in our society. We are here, backed by copious amounts of research, to tell you that over-functioning is not a badge of honor; it is the fulfillment of a capitalist ideal we were sold to make society work and businesses profitable. This is fine if we realize this and keep it in perspective so that we can keep our lives in balance. To be effective, people do not need simply to survive, they need to thrive. This means you too. If this feels too big a leap for you as a servant leader, try this framing: You need to take care of yourself to take care of others. You matter.

## Reflect on the Environment (and on Yourself as an Environment)

Scanning the work environment for patterns relating to opportunity, power, identity, connection, bias, and stale logics helps to make work more thoughtful, equitable, inclusive, and responsive. Today's leaders must know how to fully engage with a range of perspectives to understand team and workplace dynamics and how specific kinds of dynamics sediment process and silo knowledge more complexly. This requires criticality about how the organizational system works in terms of bottlenecks and enablers across the work environment (covered extensively in Chapter Three). This means *viewing yourself as an environment*, as the one who creates the organization's ethos and values. Reflecting on yourself is vital to seeing your influence and impact.

Spiritual leader Thich Nhat Hanh (2015) offers the insight that, "Many of us have been running all our lives. Practice stopping." Reflection is how we stop, or at least how we slow down for a bit to think (and feel). Reflection is the most powerful tool in a leader's toolbox. Last year, Forbes suggested that leaders think of self-reflection and improving self-awareness as part of their self-care, recommending that leaders slow down and reflect on their experiences to create space for intention, dialogue, and choice. Taking time to consider the lessons of our experiences and what others reflect to us about ourselves is a profound act of self-care. Reflective practice improves a leader's understanding of self, others, their organization, and the world. Set an intention (and alarm on your phone) to reflect every day, even if you start small— even 1 minute. You, your leadership, and your organization will benefit from it exponentially.

Create inquiry routines to support an inquiry mindset and make it sustainable. Through the practice of reflection, leaders develop new insights and skills. The goal is to situate yourself as a learner, to examine your ideologies, tacit beliefs, and implicit biases, engaging in dialogue with others to understand how they shape your professional practice with a 'beginner mind'—as if you are seeing them for the first time. An inquiry mindset requires that leaders take a constructively critical learning stance on self. This means reading yourself and others with disciplined, curious, and compassionate humility. Through self-reflection, leaders open possibilities for authentic learning and growth. An inquiry mindset helps leaders identify and upset normative knowledge hierarchies (including in their own thinking), which enables them to foster a more critical and relational learning environment.

Being a reflective leader means making a commitment to learning and growing through active reflection and dialogue with trusted thought partners. Adaptive leaders make decisions only after they have reflected on their experiences and sought out insights and perspectives from a range of people differently situated in the organization who can help improve learning. Self-reflection and dialogue create opportunities for increased self-awareness, deepened learning, and growth. The key is to dedicate time to think about yourself in ways that can challenge you to open new doors of understanding within yourself which help you understand how you impact the environment.

In his poem, "I Am Much Too Alone in This World, Yet Not Alone," poet Rainer Maria Rilke (2001) writes, "I want to unfold. Nowhere I wish to stay crooked, bent; for there I would be dishonest, untrue." Many of us feel inauthentic and disconnected at work, and it does not need to be this way. Harvard

Business School professor Chris Argyris (1980) offers the useful frame of "making the undiscussable and its undiscussability discussable" to name dynamics around why some kinds of thoughts or conversations are considered taboo in teams and organizations. The concept of 'undiscussables' helps explain why people fold in parts of ourselves 'voluntarily' within workplace dynamics that make certain topics and ideas off-limits or problematic.

Choosing to unfold aspects of ourselves that remain hidden, perhaps even to us, that constrain our ability to be in authentic relationships with ourselves and each other, is the ultimate liberation a person can experience because it means traversing shame in the process of learning and positive change. Naming undiscussables requires bravery and the cultivation of psychological safety for authentic and durable organizational learning, growth, and adaptation. Even as you drive this work in earnest, be patient with yourself and others—it takes time to develop stamina to engage inquiry and reflection skills as a practice. Model this. Inquiry practices become their own reward; they create inspiring momentum once they click. Throw the inquiry rock into the lake and make the ripples.

## Invisible Logics Drive Organizations, People, Decisions. Harness Them

Invisible logics (discussed in Chapter One) are a person's specific method of reasoning that forms the basis of their thought patterns, reasoning, and decision-making. Human beings are socialized into logics that remain invisible to us, yet guide our foundational values, our interpretations of everything including ourselves, and our thoughts and decisions—all without our conscious awareness. An inquiry mindset surfaces invisible logics and traditional notions of what constitutes valid knowledge and who is a knower by identifying and challenging traditional workplace norms as based on the pervasive imposition of Western hierarchical and linear logics that devalue non-Western-White values, knowledges, and axioms (and the people who hold them).

A leader's ability to identify and challenge the tacit value systems into which they have been socialized, which are sedimented into institutional functioning and undermine authentic connection and true collaboration, requires willingness to question our indoctrination into systems of performance and evaluation based on proscribed forms of social, cultural, and educational capital that reflect and perpetuate an imagined White male ideal. This statement is not political; it reflects real history that is now in need of updating, and understanding this seeds nimbleness in today's workscape.

Leader learning agility requires observing and adjusting one's inner meaning-making systems with present and curious humility. Ongoing self-reflection is key. Invisible logic scans are one concrete way to identify hidden biases and invisible logics that shape our mindsets, belief systems, and decision-making processes.

As a focused inquiry process, reflexive logic scans enlighten individuals, teams, and groups through surfacing subjective logics people have indexed as objective facts. The scans include the invisible logics scan, emotional labor scan, espoused theory and theory-in-use scan, deflection scan, and societal trope scan. Questioning invisible logics generates awareness of how specific logics impact thoughts, choices, and behavior—one's own and across the organization.

Work, and thus our work lives, reflect norms, meaning, values, and processes from times long ago that are no longer relevant. We know this. Media eruptions over values clashes get leaders and companies in trouble in the news daily—a clarion call for proactive and lasting change. Invisible logic work is an impactful way forward—everyone has them, they are tacit, and people surface and learn a great deal through identifying them; this in turn creates the space and understanding necessary to foreground a diverse range of knowledges, ideas, and solutions.

The identification and clearing out of old logics and behaviors are individual and collective endeavors—social constructions are given power by the collective, and individuals turn these on themselves through self-judgment without conscious agreement on their value (for more on this, we recommend *The Four Agreements* by Don Miguel Ruiz (2001), discussed in the section on tools in Chapter One). Baking these reflective processes into organizational and team practices is necessary to create maximal and sustainable impact.

## Humanize People, Hybridize Knowledge, Distribute Wisdom

Research on how COVID-19 impacts the workplace reports that growth has become a centrally important factor in employee rates of satisfaction and engagement. Leaders who are unsupportive toward the growth and professional development of their employees tend to engender negative feelings and see higher employee turnover. Leaders who lead with empathy and offer meaningful growth and professional development opportunities develop relational trust and foster a culture of transparency and inquiry to understand contexts and issues better.

To these ends, self-awareness is a foundational professional competency; it is necessary for employees to identify strengths and areas that need further development. Through tending to the cultivation of their emotional intelligence, leaders are better able to self-reflect and, in turn, to recognize their impact on others. Just as self-awareness is crucial to authenticity, sharing ideas freely and listening for understanding (rather than simply to respond or defend) help to hybridize workplace knowledge by freeing people from organizational silos—both structural and relational.

Adaptive leaders enact and support a *distributive wisdom approach* (discussed in Chapter Two), a solutionary organizational learning approach that centralizes equitable communication norms to drive integrated learning as professional development. A distributive wisdom approach decentralizes pervasive knowledge hierarchies to create openings for marginalized knowledges and wisdoms of practice to be centered. A range of knowledges and kinds of expertise are identified and uplifted through systematic inquiry-based processes and ongoing professional development. This creates opportunities for integrated knowledge and adaptive expertise development when designed and scaffolded well.

A distributive wisdom approach is an intentional approach to deepening, hybridizing, and proliferating organizational knowledge, expertise, and learning. It centralizes knowledge hybridization and shared wisdom in ways that help leaders, teams, and organizations enact equitable communication structures and processes. Adaptive leaders value insights from a range of people, understanding that 'hive mind' is the best mind. Hybridizing knowledge makes innovation more thoughtful and sustainable. To drive this, leaders model and lead humble inquiry, what organizational culture guru Edgar Schein (2013) offers as the relationally attuned process of learning others through asking questions to which you do not already know the answer to build relationships based on mutual curiosity and interest.

Humble inquiry is the enactment of an inquiry mindset with others; it requires intention, humility, emotional intelligence, care, and equity literacy. Importantly, humble inquiry becomes increasingly difficult as one's status increases. Work on and model humble inquiry as an ethic of your leadership practice to create a diffusion effect of inquiry. As lead learner, it is your widest remit to elevate equity, diversity, the identification and addressing of bias, relational trust, and authenticity. Create an ethos that invites, affirms, and integrates shared knowledge and learning as a mission mode. Remember that "everyone is an expert of their own experience" who can teach you things that you need to know to be successful and sustainable as a leader in these new times (Ravitch & Carl, 2019).

## No More Boxes, No New Normal

For decades, businesses have been encouraged to 'think outside the box' as a driving metaphor for next-generation critical thinking and innovation. However, this adage does not drive change nearly far enough because *it still centers the box*, an artifact from an old way of thinking that limits innovation. Today's adaptive leaders understand that innovation is not simply a matter of thinking outside or beyond the box; they have the knowledge, savvy, and confidence to see that *the box is a distraction and not even a relevant construct*. They know that, if the box is the departure point, their thinking remains tied to it as the origin concept. Today's workscape demands a radical departure from linear thought and habituated action and embrace of systems and spatial concepts.

Sustainable organizational change happens through seeing beyond the confines of status quo norms and habits of mind that keep organizations in default comfort zones which limit creative future building. As thinking beyond the box still centers someone else's concept framed in their language (the box), leaders must free their thoughts from outdated pre-pandemic thinking and concepts. Life has changed. The axiom of work has changed. People's needs and situations and expectations have changed. And things are still changing; society is still experiencing the aftershocks of a rolling global pandemic. We must give ourselves and each other permission to liberate the workplace from no-longer-relevant ideas and the limiting behaviors and ecosystems they foster. When we do this, the possibilities for true prosperity are endless.

Dominant logics have long functioned as the assumed center, norm, and reference point for the determination of what constitutes valid knowledge. This has bred an unquestioned human hierarchy. Most organizational logics still center dominant (White Western) constructions of value, success, and innovation, exported to the world through modernization. When people and organizations are governed by a set of rules and logics that they live within as normative, thinking without these logics, which have been the main source of certainty and comfort, can feel uncomfortable and destabilizing. Even as we experience new feelings and ideas that drive further departure from old ways of thinking and doing things, we are still adhering to the norms and rules of an old mindset, and its attendant logics still organize our thinking.

For example, the popular COVID-19 logic of 'returning to normal' or creating a 'new normal' revisits and adheres to the existing logics of the box. Returning to normal is a logic that enables society, and each of us, to avoid doing the rigorous work needed to create sustainable change, since frames and ideas that decenter dominant ideologies are kept marginal, unable to surface. This limits our individual and collective ability to take responsibility for building freedom. Ai Weiwei (2018) offers,

> The West always says, "We are free," but that is deceptive. Freedom has to assume responsibility. Freedom needs new goals and new means to achieve them. We need a new language. All this requires commitment on the part of the individual. Without that, a society cannot be free.

To be truly free, we need new language, and we also need a renewed commitment and sense of responsibility to humanize and show up for each other.

Adaptive leaders understand that there is no longer a single locality of logic, not a new box or a new normal' out there, but, rather, leverageable entrepreneurial traits and skills from which newness and innovation are ever emergent. The point is to understand that things are no longer centralized; everything looks different for everyone because meaning is contextual, subjective, and perspectival; everyone has their own individual lens for seeing the world. How solutions emerge depends on our lenses, frames, and reference points.

Adaptability looks like how you, in your role and spheres of influence, understand and create cultures of interconnectedness and make decisions to reject harmful parts of organizational culture in order to make room for and invite in new logics, values, and ways of seeing the world and the workplace. Until a true departure from dominant logics and their spread in human (de)valuation occurs, leaders and organizations will continue to reinscribe harm, often without even knowing they are doing so. We cannot do anything new, sustainable, or truly innovative when our imagining of the beyond is still based on the existing logics and practices of the box.

Adaptive leaders take a constructively critical perspective on grand, deficit narratives of individuals and groups, working to recognize how their own participation in these enactments of scarcity logics serves to limit their ability to understand and amplify a diverse range of perspectives to support knowledge hybridization. Once leaders realize how they participate in the box, even as they begin to think beyond it, they are better situated and better able to make decisions based on their clear understanding of how they are tied to the perpetuation of harmful workplace logics, practices, and policies. This acknowledgment marks a departure from old and habituated ways of thinking, creating the critical distance and space necessary for new ideas and frames to emerge.

To create adaptive and sustainable organizational change, leaders need to reconstruct processes for sharing knowledge and thinking in systems with humanizing and equitable rules. A key lesson of the pandemic is that there is no longer a validated center to refer or return to; that has been proven to be false, a mirage of history through the hand of dominance. We again share the West African proverb that tells us that, "The lion's story will never be known as long as the hunter is the one to tell it." Dominance silences and siloes. Leaders must seek out and listen to the lions in their organizations and stop praising the hunters or simply believing their versions of the story prima facie. Find and listen to the lions.

This realization and its workplace reverberations can at times create tension, discomfort, and even disequilibrium, because the box (as the center and dominant version of reality) provided a rooted locality—particularly for those of us who are White. The logic of this center is false and problematic, and it is also not shared across demographic groups given radically different experiences of society along structural equity lines. Adaptive change in this realm requires adaptation to an ongoing state of change. This is uncomfortable for those of us used to the certainty and linearity we believed our old ways of seeing the world provided. This new social moment illuminates that no one is at the center anymore—this is the lesson of the pandemic and the new axiom of work.

*So, what can leaders learn from this moment?*

*Framing is everything.* Logics produce frames for interpreting the world, and these frames delimit what we can see and how we interpret the meaning of what we see. Leaders need solutionary and constructively critical frames to drive adaptive organizational processes in the current milieu.

*Change must be adaptive, like the people who drive and enact it.* To be durable, change must be a visionary, creative, and participatory process that centers diverse knowledges and perspectives, not just traditional ones.

*Representation matters.* Every single member of an organization has valuable expertise and wisdom to share; diversity of thought and identities is an asset and a differentiator for successful organizations. Old imposing hierarchies built on socially constructed values and logics now occlude and marginalize certain kinds of expertise and are ineffective; they create workplace issues that simply do not need to exist. Old status quo logics must go. Like the box. Create the next thing.

## Final Thoughts

This is a complex and hopeful time. As a leader, you are called upon to do and be a lot of things for a lot of people, including yourself. As precarity and change become an enduring reality, the Flux 5 framework helps leaders to chart and light the path forward, bring everyone with them, and create growth in diffusion effect. Luminary Yung Pueblo offers a vision of where such bravery can lead us as we enter the third year of a global pandemic:

> We live in a unique time, where fear-driven and hateful emotions are coming to the surface so that they can be completely released, so that we can create a new world where institutionalized forms of harm are no longer a factor in our lives—as people learn that it benefits them to stop harming themselves and others, our world will become less harm-filled. The same way it works for the individual, so does it also work for the collective of humanity—we can't heal what is ignored, nor can we live happily and freely if we continue running away from our own darkness.
>
> Humans affect one another deeply, in ways that the world at large is just beginning to understand. When we begin healing ourselves it sets off waves that connect us to the healing of those who have healed in the past and the future. When we heal ourselves, it gives strength to those who need more support to take on their own personal healing journey. What we do reverberates throughout time and space—like a rock thrown into a lake, the circles it creates move in all directions.
>
> Personally, my faith is in people. Our courage to turn inward in the hopes of uncovering and releasing all that stands in our way of becoming beings of unconditional love is what will bring harmony and peace to our world. Unity with those around us is most possible when we become internally whole and loving. Wisdom more easily flows through us when our minds and hearts are no longer reacting to the suffering of everyday life—this does not mean that it makes us cold, it means that we learn to respond to the changes in life with love, patience, and kindness without causing ourselves misery, we learn to respond to life as opposed to blindly reacting to it.
>
> *(Yung Pueblo, 2016)*

The goal is for all of us to live in this sense of hope and interconnectedness. In these unusual times all over the world, leaders are called upon to imagine and lead complex adaptive change, to engage flux. This means distributing the transformative leadership load throughout organizations with fidelity to equity, inclusion, and humanization. It also means reflecting on what needs to be different for your organization to live out its espoused values across its structures, processes, and actions. As we close, we recall Arundhati Roy's (2020) clarion call for leader-led change:

> Whatever it is, coronavirus has made the mighty kneel and brought the world to a halt like nothing else could. Our minds are still racing back and forth, longing for a return to "normality", trying to stitch our future to our past and refusing to acknowledge the rupture. But the rupture exists. And in the midst of this terrible despair, it offers us a chance to rethink the doomsday machine we have built for ourselves. Nothing could be worse than a return to normality.

Just as change offers opportunities for learning and growth, ruptures offer opportunities for deep repair. Now is the time for leaders to engage in their deepest and most catalytic growth work—for themselves and those they serve. Inquiry, humanization, systems, entrepreneurship, and equity are necessary mindsets to make work a place of solutionary and leading-edge thought, practice, and participation. This is what it means to be a portal, fostering the conditions for transformational growth, learning, and adaptive change. This time has taught us, most of all, that our liberation is bound up in each other; it is time we choose to humanize ourselves and each other. Leaders must serve as night lanterns, illuminating our way forward in and beyond these dark times.

# REFERENCES

Abbott, S. (2018). *The Weight of History*. Springer.

Acaroglu, L. (2017). *Disruptive Design Handbook. A Method for Activating Positive Social Change by Design*. Disrupt Design.

Adichie, C. N. (2009). *The Danger of a Single Story*. TedTalk.

Arao, B. & Clemens, K. (2013). From Safe Spaces to Brave Spaces: A New Way to Frame Dialogue around Diversity and Social Justice. In *The Art of Effective Facilitation: Reflections from Social Justice Educators*. Landreman, Stylus Publishing, 135–150.

Argyris, C. (1980). Making the Undiscussable and Its Undiscussability Discussable. *Public Administration Review, 40*(3), 205–213. https://doi.org/10.2307/975372

Argyris, C. (2004). *Reasons and Rationalizations: The Limits to Organizational Knowledge*. Oxford University Press.

Argyris, C. & Schön, D. (1978). *Organizational Learning: A Theory of Action Perspective*. Addison-Wesley.

Augustine, of Hippo, Saint, 354-430. (1940–1949). *The Confessions of Saint Augustine*. Peter Pauper Press.

Ballou, H. *Hosea Ballou Papers, 1810–1890., bMS 366*. Harvard Divinity School Library, Harvard University.

Bhabha, H. K. (2004). *The Location of Culture*. Routledge.

Brown, A. M. (2017). *Emergent Strategy: Shaping Change Shaping Worlds*. AK Press.

Brown, B. (2019). BRAVING [YouTube]. www.youtube.com/watch?v=0SqFiTeka_I

Bryk, A. & Schneider, B. (2002). *Trust in Schools: A Core Resource for Improvement*. Russell Sage Foundation.

Caird, S. (2013). General Measure of Enterprising Tendency Test. www.get2test.net. 10.13140/RG.2.1.4243.7520

Clark, T. R. (2020). *The 4 Stages of Psychological Safety: Defining the Path to Inclusion and Innovation*. Berrett-Koehler.

Cochran-Smith, M. & Lytle, S. L. (2009). *Inquiry as Stance: Practitioner Research for the Next Generation*. Teachers College Press.

Crary, M. (2017). Working from Dominant Identity Positions: Reflections from Diversity-Aware White People about Their Cross-Race Work Relationships. *Journal of Applied Behavioral Science, 53*(2), 290–316.

Crenshaw, K. (2023). *On Intersectionality: Essential Writings*. The New Press.

Crenshaw, K. W. (1994). Mapping the Margins: Intersectionality, Identity Politics, and Violence against Women of Color. In Martha Albertson Fineman & Rixanne Mykitiuk, Eds., *The Public Nature of Private Violence*. Routledge, pp. 93–118.

Csikszentmihalyi, M. (1996). *Creativity: Flow and the Psychology of Discovery and Invention*. Harper Collins.

Deloitte. (2021). *The Equity Imperative Report*. Deloitte.

Duckworth, A. (2016). *Grit: The Power of Passion and Perseverance*. Scribner.

Dweck, C. S. (2008). *Mindset*. Ballantine Books.

Eberhardt, J. L. (2019). *Biased: Uncovering the Hidden Prejudice That Shapes What We See, Think, and Do*. Viking, Penguin Random House.

Edwards, J. (2015). Personal communication with Dr. Howard Stevenson.

Einstein, A. (1946). Telegram quoted in the *New York Times*, May 25.

Feltman C., Hammond S. A., Hammond R., Marshall A., & Bendis K. (2009). *The Thin Book of Trust: An Essential Primer for Building Trust at Work*. Thin Book.

Forrester, J. W. (1961). *Industrial Dynamics*. M.I.T. Press.

Frankl, V. E. (1946). *Ein psycholog erlebt das konzentrationslager*. Verlag für Jugend und Volk.

Frankl, V. E. (1977). *Trotzdem ja zum leben sagen: Ein psychologe erlebt das konzentrationslage*. Kösel.

Freire, P. (2000). *Pedagogy of Freedom*. Rowman & Littlefield.

Friday, C. (2019). *Curiosity as Power*. Self-Published.

Gallup. (2018). Gallup's Approach to Culture: Building a Culture that Drives Performance. http://acrip.co/contenidos-acrip/gallup/2020/noviembre/gallup-perspective-building-a-culture-that-drives-performance.pdf

González, N., Moll, L., & Amanti, C. (Eds.). (2005). *Funds of Knowledge: Theorizing Practices in Households, Communities and Classrooms*. Erlbaum.

Guilles, W. (2015). State of Entrepreneurship 2015 Address. Ewing Marion Kauffman Foundation.

Hanisch, C. (1970). The Personal Is Political. In S. Firestone & A. Koedt, Eds., *Notes from the Second Year: Women's Liberation: Major writings of the radical feminists*. Radical Feminism, 76–78.

Heifetz R., Grashow A., & Linsky M. (2009a). Leadership in a (Permanent) Crisis. *Harvard Business Review*, 87(7-8), 62–69, 153. PMID:19630256

Heifetz, R. A., Linsky, M., & Grashow, A. (2009b). *The Practice of Adaptive Leadership*. Harvard Business Review Press.

Held Evans, R. (2018). *Inspired: Slaying Giants, Walking on Water, and Loving the Bible Again*. Thomas Nelson.

Hochschild A. R. (1983). *The Managed Heart: Commercialization of Human Feeling*. University of California Press.

hooks, b. (1994). *Teaching to Transgress: Education as the Practice of Freedom*. Routledge.

James, E. H. & Wooten, L. P. (2011). Crisis Leadership and Why it Matters. *The European Financial Review*. December–January.

James, W. (1890). *The Principles of Psychology*. Henry Holt.

Kafka, F. (1996). *The Metamorphosis and Other Stories*. (S. Appelbaum, Trans.). Dover Publications.

Kanfer, R. (1992). Work Motivation: New Directions in Theory and Research. *International Review of Industrial & Organizational Psychology*, 7, 1–53.

Khalifa, M. (2018). *Culturally Responsive School Leadership*. Harvard Education Press.

Khilji, S. (2020). Making Diversity Work: Rethinking Human Nature to Humanize Organizations. *Medium*. https://shaistakhilji.medium.com/making-diversity-work-rethinking-human-nature-to-humanize-organizations-7bfe586c756c

Knight, F. (1921). *Risk, Uncertainty and Profit*. Houghton Mifflin.

LeGrand, E. & Ravitch, S. M. (2022). The "Great Resignation" as Research Context: Educational, Organizational, and Individual Realities in Flux. Sage MethodSpace.

Leutner, F., Ahmetoglu, G., Akhtar, R., & Chamorro-Premuzic, T. (2014). The Relationship between the Entrepreneurial Personality and the Big Five Personality Traits. *Personality and Individual Differences*, *63*, 58–63. ISSN 0191-8869, https://doi.org/10.1016/j.paid.2014.01.042

Levin, N. (2015). Is It Time for a Graceful Exit? NancyLevin.com. https://nancylevin.com/is-it-time-for-a-graceful-exit/

Lorde, A. (1984). *Sister Outsider: Essays and Speeches*. Crossing Press.

McHenry, T. (2020). *Bias in Bias Out: A Microsoft White Paper*. Microsoft.

Meadows. L. (2020). The Equity Mindset: From Activities to Function. *Forbes*. www.forbes.com/sites/forbescoachescouncil/2020/12/01/the-equity-mindset-from-activities-to-function/?sh=41193d252cb8

Mescon, T. & van Rest, E. (2021). Entrepreneurship Is an Opportunity for Education. Association for the Advancement of Colleges and Schools of Business (AACSB). www.aacsb.edu/insights/articles/2021/03/entrepreneurship-is-an-opportunity-for-education

Nakkula, M. J. & Ravitch, S. M. (1998). *Matters of Interpretation: Reciprocal Transformation in Therapeutic and Developmental Relationships with Youth*. Jossey-Bass.

Neck, H. M. (2010). Idea Generation. In B. Bygrave & A. Zacharakis, Eds., *Portable MBA in Entrepreneurship*. Wiley.

Norton, R. (2013). *The Power of Starting Something Stupid: How to Crush Fear, Make Dreams Happen, and Live without Regret*. Shadow Mountain.

Pak, K. & Ravitch, S. M. (2021). *Critical Leadership Praxis for Educational and Social Change*. Teachers College Press.

Petriglieri, G. (2020). The Psychology behind Effective Crisis Leadership. *Harvard Business Review*. https://hbr.org/2020/04/the-psychology-behind-effective-crisis-leadership

Pink, D. H. (2006). *A Whole New Mind: Why Right-Brainers Will Rule the Future*. Riverhead Books.

Prather, H. (1972). *I touch the earth, the earth Touches Me*. Main Street Books.

Proust, M. & Milly J. (2003). *La prisonnière* (3rd ed., reviewed and updated). Flammarion.

Pueblo, Yung. (2016, November 9). We Live in a Unique Time, where Fear-Driven and Hateful Emotions Are Coming to the Surface .... Facebook. www.facebook.com/yungpueblo/photos/we-live-in-a-unique-time-where-fear-driven-and-hateful-emotions-are-coming-to-th/1266563546741970/

Rauch, A. (2014). Predictions of Entrepreneurial Behavior: A Personality Approach. In E. Chell & M. Karatas-Ozkan, Eds., *Handbook of Research on Small Business and Entrepreneurship*. Edward Elgar, 165–183.

Ravitch, S. M. (2020). Why Teaching through Crisis Requires a Radical New Mindset: Introducing Flux Pedagogy. *Harvard Business Publishing: Education*, August 12.

Ravitch, S. M. & Carl, N. M. (2019). *Applied Research for Sustainable Change: A Guidebook for Leaders*. Harvard Education Press.

Ravitch S. M. & Carl, M. N. (2021). *Qualitative Research: Bridging the Conceptual, Theoretical, and Methodological* (2nd ed.). Sage.

Ravitch, S. M. & Kannan, C. A. (Eds.). (2022). *Flux Leadership: Real-Time Inquiry for Humanizing Educational Change.* Teachers College Press.

Richo, D. (2019). *Triggers: How We Can Stop Reacting and Start Healing.* Shambhala.

Rilke, R. M. (2001). *The Book of Hours: Prayers to a Lowly God.* (A. S. Kidder, Trans.). Northwestern University Press.

Robinson, P. B., Stimpson, D. V., Huefner, J. C., & Hunt, H. K. (1991). An Attitude Approach to the Prediction of Entrepreneurship. *Entrepreneurship Theory and Practice, 15,* 13–31.

Rogers, M. E. (2003). *Diffusion of Innovations* (5th ed.). Free Pass.

Roy, A. (2020). The Pandemic Is a Portal. *Financial Times,* April 3.

Rukeyser, M. (1968). Käthe Kollwitz. In *The Speed of Darkness.* Random House.

Ruiz, D. M. (2001). *The Four Agreements.* Amber-Allen.

Rushdie, S. (1991). One Thousand Days in a Balloon. *The New York Times,* December 12.

Sartre, J.-P. (2003). *Being and Nothingness* (H. E. Barnes, Trans.; 2nd ed.). Routledge.

Schein, E. (2013). *Humble Inquiry: The Gentle Art of Asking Instead of Telling.* Berrett-Koehler.

Sen, A. (2004). *Rationality and Freedom.* Harvard University Press.

Senge, P. (2012). *Schools That Learn: A Fifth Discipline Fieldbook for Educators, Parents and Everyone who Cares about Education.* Doubleday.

Serrat, O. (2017). The Five Whys Technique. In *Knowledge Solutions.* Springer, Singapore.

Shulman L. S. & Wilson S. M. (2004). *The Wisdom of Practice: Essays on Teaching Learning and Learning to Teach* (1st ed.). Jossey-Bass.

Stevenson, H. C. (2014). *Promoting Racial Literacy in Schools: Differences That Make a Difference.* Teachers College Press.

Sull, D., Sull, C., & Zwieg, B. (2022). Toxic Culture Is Driving the Great Resignation. *MIT Sloan Management Review.*

Taylor, S. R. (2021). *The Body Is Not an Apology* (2nd ed.). Berrett-Koehler.

Thich Nhat Hanh (2015). *The Heart of the Buddha's Teaching: Transforming Suffering into Peace, Joy, and Liberation.* Harmony.

Torrance, W. & Rauch, J. (2013). *Entrepreneurship Education Comes of Age on Campus.* Kauffman Foundation.

Valencia, R. R. (2010). *Dismantling Contemporary Deficit Thinking: Educational Thought and Practice.* Routledge.

Vygotsky, L. S. (1978). *Mind in Society: The Development of Higher Psychological Processes.* Harvard University Press.

Waheed, N. (2013). *Salt.* Nayyirah Waheed.

Weiwei, A. (2018). *Humanity.* Princeton University Press.

Winnicott, D. (1960). UK Essays. Holding and Containing. www.ukessays.com/essays/psychology/holding-and-containing-winnicott.php?vref=1

Watson, L. (1994). The affirmation of indigenous values in a colonial education system. In P.G. Stone and R. MacKenzie, Eds., *The Excluded Past: Archaeology in Education.* Routledge Chapman & Hall.

Zhao, H., Seibert, S. E., & Lumpkin, G. T. (2010). The Relationship of Personality to Entrepreneurial Intentions and Performance: A Meta-Analytic Review. *Journal of Management, 36,* 381–404. https://doi.org/10.1177/0149206309335187

# INDEX